EX LIBRIS

MUSIC
A CRASH COURSE

MUSIC
A CRASH COURSE
MARCUS WEEKS

WATSON-GUPTILL
PUBLICATIONS
New York

First published in the United States in 1999
by Watson-Guptill Publications, a division of
BPI Communications, Inc., 1515 Broadway,
New York, NY 10036

Library of Congress Catalog Card Number: 99-61086

ISBN 0-8230-0978-5

*This book was conceived, designed,
and produced by*
THE IVY PRESS LIMITED
2/3 St Andrews Place
Lewes, East Sussex, BN7 1UP

Art Director: PETER BRIDGEWATER
Editorial Director: SOPHIE COLLINS
Designer: JANE LANAWAY
Project Editor: HELEN CLEARY
Editor: PETER NICKOL
DTP Designer: CHRIS LANAWAY
Illustrations: RACHEL FULLER
Picture Researcher: VANESSA FLETCHER

Printed and bound in Hong Kong by
Hong Kong Graphic and Printing

1 2 3 4 5 6 7 8 9 10/08 07 06 05 04 03 02 01 00 99

This book is typeset in Bauer Bodoni 8/11

DEDICATION

For Kiersten, with love

Contents

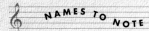

NAMES TO NOTE

All those composers there isn't room for in the main text, but whose music is often played, or has some claim to fame.

Introduction

So, what's this Crash Course all about? "Western Art Music" if you want to be pedantic; "serious" music if you really must; but "classical" music is what most of us call it. That's just about everything that has its roots in the European tradition, and isn't pop, jazz, folk, or opera (all of which deserve Crash Courses of their own). Big subject.

The course is in the form of a concise history, in (near enough) chronological order. Each two-page spread deals with a particular period or style, giving the lowdown on all the major composers and their music. There's no need for any previous musical knowledge—there are a few "digressions" littered around explaining technical stuff where it seems appropriate, and a glossary of musical terms at the back to help

Claudio Monteverdi produced groundbreaking new music.

" ☆ "

Starred Boxes

These boxes contain fascinating facts or amusing anecdotes that you don't really need to know—but what the heck, it's all a bit of fun.

TO WATCH

WORKS

These are the pieces you really should listen to if you get the chance—the best known, most often heard, most typical of a particular genre, or just my particular favorites.

TO WATCH

WORKS

you decipher the sort of jargon you might meet in reviews, programs, sleeve notes, and intermission discussions at the bar.

Above all, it's intended as a listeners' guide, especially for those who may have been frightened off by the snobbishness of the concert-going élite and the stuffiness of the musical establishment. Ideally it should help you to really enjoy, rather than just appreciate, the music.

All the same, you can't expect to like everything, and I apologize if I wax lyrical on something that you hate. I also apologize if I've left out any of your particular favorites—sadly, there isn't room for everything.

I suppose I ought to apologize for the dreadful puns, too, but I'm not going to.

Wolfgang Amadeus Mozart—classic stuff.

Boxes
... like this give additional info connected with the stuff on the rest of the spread—filling in the background, rhapsodizing on a theme, or anything else that I think might help you enjoy the music or impress friends at dinner parties. And, to put the music into its historical perspective, there's a timeline at the top of each page.

HELPFUL HINTS
Helpful hints to enhance your listening pleasure, give shortcuts to understanding what's going on, or clarify confusions. Particularly useful with less familiar or "difficult" music.

Marcus Weeks

Franz Liszt—Romantic composer, pianist, and international superstar.

MARCUS WEEKS

30,000–10,000 BC
Bone pipes and rock paintings found in sites across Europe, North Africa, and Western Asia testify to Stone Age music making.

c.600 BC Phoenician sailors circumnavigate Africa on the orders of Pharaoh II of Egypt. They take over two years to complete their journey.

325 BC Alexander's admiral Nearchus describes Indian reeds "that produce honey, although there are no bees"—the first reference to sugar cane.

BC~AD 600

In the Beginning
Musical Prehistory

Nobody can say for certain how music started. Possibly storytellers started to sing their tales to make them easier to memorize, or maybe a cavedweller somewhere noticed an interesting sound as two rocks hit each other, or as the wind blew through the reeds. Perhaps it was later than that, when hunters heard the distinctive twang of their bows. What we do know is that music was an integral part of people's lives even before we gave up our nomadic lifestyle— primitive whistles have been found from around 40,000 BC, and there are cave paintings featuring musicians from around 18,000 BC.

In classical myth, Orpheus captured Eurydice's heart with his musical skills.

There is also a great deal of evidence of music making in the ancient civilizations of Mesopotamia, China, and Egypt, through paintings and contemporary writings. Some of the instruments they played have survived to the present. Their harps, lyres, pipes, horns, and trumpets were quite sophisticated and were probably used in religious and court ceremonies. We've only the vaguest idea of what the music sounded like, however, because none of it was written down. From our vantage point, this was the primordial musical soup from which "classical" music evolved.

IT'S ALL GREEK TO ME

Music was also important to the ancient Greeks—in fact the word "music" comes from the Greek word *mousike* (which was used to describe dance and poetry as well as music). *Mousike* was not just for ceremonial use, but also part of entertainments such as theater, poetry, and dance.

Pythagoras

It is well known that Pythagoras (c.580–c.500 BC) was fascinated not only by mathematics; he was also keen on music. In his quest to explain the "harmony of the spheres" (a sort of Ancient Greek Theory of Everything), he experimented with vibrating strings (like those on a guitar) and discovered mathematical relationships between notes of the scale. He is also credited with giving letter-names to the notes, and is looked on as being the forefather of modern musical theory.

320 BC A Ptolemaic inscription describes wooden poles capped with copper sheaths to "cut the lightning out of the sky."

110 BC Romans farm oysters—the first known example of Western efforts to cultivate seafood.

AD 92 Roman historian Tacitus describes songs in which the Germanic peoples celebrate their gods and their mythical past and record their history.

This is the first hard evidence we have of art for art's sake, at least as far as music is concerned. Luckily for us, the Greeks also wrote a fair amount about their music, especially the theory of music, so we have a pretty good idea of how they thought, even if we can't tell exactly what they played.

The ancient Romans liked their music too, rather more robustly than the Greeks, and they were particularly fond of instrumental bands as part of their games and orgies. Possibly because they were so busy living it up and enjoying themselves, they didn't leave a lot of musical literature for posterity. They did, however, leave a significant but negative legacy, in that the emerging Christian church reacted to their decadent hedonism by rejecting instrumental music completely, adopting instead an austere style of vocal music. And as the church had a virtual monopoly on Europe's medieval cultural life, that's where the story of Western classical music really begins.

Oral Traditions

It's not just this very early music that didn't get written down. In fact, until very recently, most music other than Western classical music has been passed down orally: just about everything from rural folk music through jazz to the court and religious music outside the European tradition. And that's a lot of music.

This Roman fresco (c. 450 BC) shows servants and musicians making music. They weren't so keen on writing the stuff down, though.

c.524 Boethius, Roman scholar, philosopher, and translator, is executed. His treatise *De Institutione Musica* will be a standard textbook of the Middle Ages.

c.624 The Koran's third part is composed. Though intended to be read aloud, it influences written language and marks the beginning of Arab literature.

644 Tokoyonomushi, a new religion, springs up in Japan. Devotees worship a large worm, get drunk, dance in the streets, and give away all their money.

300~800
Pope Gregory Immortalized
Medieval Church Music

Gregory I, credited with the introduction of the Gregorian chant.

The so-called Dark Ages could be called the Quiet Ages, so little is really known about what people were playing and singing. It's more than likely that folk music of all sorts was thriving despite the church's disapproval. There was probably a good deal of music in the royal courts too. There's no way of knowing what most of it was like, because only the church had a means of writing it down.

The Importance of the Church in Classical Music

Western classical music evolved from a very church-dominated culture. Even now, the bulk of classical choral music is to sacred texts, and most composers (even some atheists and agnostics) have written in forms such as the mass. Nowadays, it's as likely you'll hear the great choral works in a concert hall as in a church, but—if you can endure the often spartan seating—a church setting is the best place to appreciate them.

The system of notation for church music was, however, pretty rudimentary: a kind of musical shorthand used as an *aide-mémoire* for singers. It consisted of a set of graphic symbols, called neumes, representing different notes and common patterns of notes, which were used to write down the various tunes associated with the different parts of the mass. These tunes, which were originally passed orally from one generation to the next and probably had their origins in Greek songs and Jewish ritual chants, are known as plainsong, or plainchant.

Each region had its own versions of plainsong. The control freaks of the church's hierarchy weren't too happy about this regional autonomy, so in the fourth century they set about some sort of standardization. *ST. AMBROSE*, Bishop of Milan (c. 340–397), was one of the first to codify plainchants, laying down the law for what is now known as Ambrosian chant.

650-750 The Lindisfarne Gospels in Northumberland and the Irish *Book of Kells* are embellished with interlacing patterns and Mediterranean-style figures.

680 The modern numerical system, using number symbols including zero and place values, is in use in Southeastern Asia.

750 The Arabian government moves to Baghdad. Music is highly valued there—a sought-after singer receives 10,000 pieces of silver per month.

GREGORIAN CHANT

Then along came *POPE GREGORY* (ruled 590–604), who added a few more standard chants and established music schools in the Roman church, setting himself up for immortality as the founder of Gregorian chant. Trouble is, what we call Gregorian chant today may not have much to do with him—it probably dates from around 800 and is Frankish in origin. Well, even musicologists make mistakes.

Nevertheless, all the church music of the early medieval period has certain characteristics

A manuscript of a seventh-century chant. The music is written above the text, using neumes.

in common. It is based on a set of melodies to be used in the various sections of the mass, it is exclusively vocal, and it is sung in unison—all the singers sing the same notes together, without harmony or accompaniment. Sounds dull? Well, austere maybe, but give it a try. It's certainly very spiritual, and at its best sublime. With the specific plainchants and the timeless quality of the music, it must have seemed like nothing could ever be different. But an Italian monk unwittingly provided the means for profound change...

Singing in the reign of Pope Gregory was usually the job of choirs of monks.

> **HELPFUL HINTS**
> The Mass.
> The central part of the Christian service is the mass, and it remains one of the most important frameworks for sacred music in the classical repertoire. So, it's useful to know the form. It has a core of six sections (known as the "Ordinary"), which always have the same text:
> *KYRIE*
> *GLORIA*
> *CREDO*
> *SANCTUS AND BENEDICTUS*
> *AGNUS DEI*
> *ITE MISSA EST (OR BENEDICAMUS DOMINO)*
> Added to these are optional and variable texts (known as the "Proper"), which may include:
> *INTROIT*
> *GRADUAL*
> *ALLELUIA (OR TRACT)*
> *SEQUENCE*
> *OFFERTORY*
> *COMMUNION*

1000 Explosive grenades and bombs are in use in China, the first country known to have developed gunpowder.

1022 Japan's greatest novel, *The Tale of Genji*, is written by a woman, Lady Murasaki.

1036 Modern musical notation is pioneered by Guido d'Arezzo, who also invents the "great scale."

1030~1050
On the Right Lines
The Birth of Modern Notation

The main feature of classical music that distinguishes it from the other music—a precise system of notation—was surprisingly late in coming. The first major step toward it was the adoption, some time in the tenth century, of a horizontal line representing a fixed pitch, on or around which the neumes were written. But the breakthrough came about a hundred years later, when some bright spark thought of adding a few more lines.

Handy music theory, invented by Guido D'Arezzo. Sleeve notes included.

That bright spark was *Guido d'Arezzo* (c.995–after 1033), an Italian monk, teacher, and music theorist. Although we can't be sure that he invented everything he's credited with, he certainly established the use of several innovations, explaining them all in a comprehensive treatise on music, *Micrologus*, in about 1030.

In *Micrologus*, as well as describing the plainsong of the time, Guido set out a method of naming the notes of the scale with syllables from a well-known Latin plainchant (a mnemonic that survives today as the sol-fa system), and an ingenious way of using the parts of the hand to teach music theory (the "Guidonian Hand"); but most importantly, he proposed a system of writing music on several parallel horizontal lines—what we now call the staff (or stave).

staff

neumelike notes

Illuminated manuscript of a Latin text set to music on a four-line staff.

c.1040 Lady Godiva rides naked through the streets of Coventry, England, to persuade her husband to remit oppressive taxes.

1042–95 St. Mark's is constructed in Venice using a cross plan (Greek) with a central dome and four surrounding domes (Byzantine).

1054 The Chinese record the sighting of a supernova (the Crab nebula); it is so bright, it can be seen by day.

TAKE FIVE

After experiments with four and six lines, a five-line staff was settled on, and modern musical notation had arrived. This brilliantly simple refinement to existing notation had shattering implications. For the first time, the pitch of every note could be precisely indicated, and music could be recorded for posterity. What's more, music could now be published and disseminated much more widely, without the tedious business of learning by rote.

True, there were drawbacks: it took a while to devise a way of showing the rhythm of the notes, and the church held a monopoly on all forms of writing.

Before Guido, divine guidance was sometimes necessary to decipher the music.

Notation As a Tool for Teaching and Performing

Try to bear in mind that the idea of writing new music was alien to the medieval church. For Guido and his contemporaries, music consisted of the traditional chants which had been passed down from antiquity (and certainly not the Godless stuff the peasants were singing and playing). Notation was a method of preserving them, teaching them, and ensuring their correct performance. But Guido's invention also helped a new breed of musician—the composer.

Notation was an aid to teaching.

Other Systems of Notation

Guido's staff notation was pretty successful in superseding older and more exotic systems, but didn't quite replace them completely. Another of his inventions, still used in some vocal music, is the syllables *ut, re, mi, fa, so,* and *la* (nowadays *do, re, mi, fa, so, la,* plus *si* or *ti*) known as solmization or the sol-fa system. Another thing you might see is tablature: a sort of diagram showing instrumentalists how to play particular notes, used in lute music and still surviving for guitarists.

That included music, so very little secular music was written down for some while. Nevertheless, this was a giant leap forward for music, opening up entirely new possibilities. In fact, once staff notation caught on, European music went through a period of profound change that would have been previously impossible.

Digression: The Dots

How Music Is Notated, and
Some Other Technical Stuff

So, Guido d'Arezzo came up with a system of writing music, which is much the same as the one used today. Okay—so how is music written today? Perhaps here's as good a place as any to have a look at music notation and explain a few of the terms associated with it, without getting too technical.

Guido d'Arezzo, pioneer of musical notation.

Let's start off with something we've come across already, the five lines (and four spaces) that the notes are written on, the staff (or stave). At the beginning of each staff is a symbol, the clef, which shows what pitch those lines represent—in other words, how high or low the notes are. For example, the treble clef (the one that looks like a stylized **&**) indicates that the second line up is the note G, while the bass clef (the one like a backward C with two dots) indicates that the second line down is an F. From these fixed points, we can work out the pitches of all the other notes on the staff.

Now, if you have a look at example 1, you'll see how this is done: each note has a letter name, from A to G, and each consecutive letter-named note occupies the next line or space up—pretty smart, huh? Extra little lines for individual notes (they're called leger lines) can be used where the staff doesn't reach, like the C in the example between the two staffs (imaginatively called middle C).

But that's not all. The notes A to G correspond to the white notes on the piano keyboard, but what about the black notes? Well, The notes of the treble and bass clefs with their letter names.

EXAMPLE 1

A B C D E F G A B C C D E F G A B C D E

EXAMPLE 2

whole note

half notes

quarter notes

eighth notes

sixteenth notes

dotted half note

= 3 quarter notes

Note lengths.

this is where sharps and flats come in. If a written note is preceded by a sharp (♯) then this indicates the very next note up, and if it's preceded by a flat (♭), it means the very next note down. Five times out of seven this means a black note (really!—try it for yourself). The sharps and flats can be canceled later by using a natural sign (♮).

I GOT RHYTHM

Now, how do we show the duration of those notes, the rhythm? Simple: the shape of the note denotes its length, and as a general rule, the more ink used, the shorter the note. Take a look at example 2. The whole note is twice as long as the half note, which is twice as long as the quarter note, and so on. A little dot after a note makes it half as long again—so a dotted half note is as long as three quarter notes (you work it out!). There's even a set of signs called rests to show different lengths of silence. For ease of reading, and to show where the main beat lies, the staff is divided into bars by vertical barlines. You can see all this in example 3.

Try to pick out the things you've learned in this short piece.

EXAMPLE 3

key signature

double barline

quarter rest

barline

half rest

1000 Sei Shonagon, lady-in-waiting to the Japanese Empress Sadako, starts to compile her *Pillow-book* with sharp observations of contemporary life.

1121 Theologian-philosopher Peter Abelard is driven into exile by professional and personal calamity. Abelard and Héloise will join the list of doomed lovers.

1162 Chancellor Thomas Becket becomes Archbishop of Canterbury. Knights loyal to Henry II will murder him in eight years.

1000~1300

The Devil Has the Best Tunes
Medieval Music Outside the Church

Although the vast majority of early medieval music that has survived is sacred music, we mustn't assume that musical activity was centered on the church. Far from it. Quite apart from folk music, which seems to thrive in every era, there were a huge number of professional musicians who traveled around Europe entertaining at the courts of the nobility. Many of them came from the educated social classes, and, luckily for us, a few had learned how to write their music on paper, albeit in a rudimentary fashion.

From the few surviving manuscripts, and from contemporary accounts of life at court, we get a very different picture from that given by church music of the time. Most important, this was music for entertainment, not spiritual edification, and they knew how to enjoy themselves in medieval courts. Not for them the church's killjoy chanting—this was the golden age of courtly love songs, often accompanied on the harp or lute, and there was even instrumental music for dancing. Much more fun.

But that didn't mean that their music was in any way lowbrow. The minstrels who performed this music were well respected as poets and musicians, and their

> **" ★ "**
>
> *I Spy*
>
> Some minstrels felt the need for a little extra excitement, not to mention a little extra cash, and found themselves ideally placed, traveling from one feudal court to another, to take up an interesting sideline—espionage. The wine often flowed freely when the music was playing, and minstrels were close enough to the noblemen to pick up quite a few useful tidbits…

Music was important to the medieval courts of Europe.

1071 Guillaume, Count of Poitiers is born—the first troubadour whose songs will survive.

1180 The first reference to a windmill with vertical sails is made in Europe.

1192 Richard the Lionheart, imprisoned in Austria on his return from the Third Crusade, is found by his troubadour friend Blondel singing the song they composed together.

Jongleurs and Jugglers

The bands of entertainers that toured Europe were not just musicians and poets. There were acrobats, storytellers, and jugglers too. The French word *jongleur*, used to describe minstrels in the early Middle Ages, is related to the word juggler, and it's quite likely that at one time they were one and the same thing—all-around entertainers available for classy medieval dinner parties.

work was an expression of noble sentiments, more sensuous than bawdy. In fact, by the thirteenth century these singer-songwriters were so well established, they were beginning to influence music in the church—as we shall soon see.

Minstrels made a good living from the feudal courts.

A WANDERING MINSTREL

There were many different names for these minstrels, depending on where they came from and when. For instance, there were *goliards* (irreverent scholars who went around lampooning the church), *jongleurs* (early French minstrels, famous for their epic ballads). *Minnesingers* (thirteenth-century German minstrels who were members of the aristocracy), and *scops* (Anglo-Saxon versions of exactly the same thing). There were also the *trouvères*—they came from northern France—and the better-known troubadours from southern France. The troubadours in particular developed song forms based on the poetic forms of the time, such as the *rondeau* and *virelai*, setting their own poetry to music (using their own language, the *langue d'oc*, not Latin), and establishing a tradition of French *chanson* that can be traced in one form or another to the present day.

1154 When Henry II's wife Eleanor of Aquitaine introduces cheap French wine, the English wine industry starts to decline.

1163 The church attempts to discourage the practice of dismembering and boiling down the bodies of dead Crusaders to transport them back home.

1200-1220 Wolfram von Eschenbach writes *Parzifal*, the best-known medieval German romance based on the legend of Perceval and the Holy Grail.

1150~1290

At Last—a Composer!
The Beginnings of Polyphony

Meanwhile, back in the church, there were some dramatic developments. Gregorian chant, sung in unison without accompaniment, had an unusual austere beauty but wasn't exactly easy on the ear. Monophony (or monody), as this single-line music is called, was on the way out, and the rot had set in as early as the ninth century. By the time Guido's groundbreaking treatise appeared, church music was crying out for reform, and his innovative notation allowed a new generation of musicians to inject new life into plainsong.

Previously thought of as diabolical, instruments gradually crept in to accompany the polyphony of the late Middle Ages. The seated player is holding a "portative" (portable organ).

HEARING VOICES

Listening to polyphonic music is like that optical illusion where you either see two faces or a vase, but never both. If you listen to one line you miss the others, but if you listen to the whole you can't always pick out the individual melodies. That's the beauty of polyphony, and why it bears repeated listening. It never sounds the same twice, and constantly engages your attention.

The first rumblings came, appropriately, from the addition of a bass line to the plainchant. Previously the tunes had been sung by tenors, the higher of the male voices (no women's voices in these choirs—heaven forbid!). But they were rather high for the basses, so, some time in the ninth century, somebody had the bright idea of singing the same tune four or five notes lower. Lo and behold, two-part harmony had been invented! This parallel harmony was known as organum, and it really spiced up the plainchant, giving it a new lease on life. By the eleventh century, a third voice had been added above the tenor, and the seed of a new style, polyphony, had been sown.

As sacred music became more complex, there was a greater need to write it down—it wasn't so easy to pass on complicated music orally—and whoever wrote it down could be a bit more creative and dictate

1200-1400 The Alhambra, a citadel and palace, is built overlooking Granada, the finest exampl of Islamic decorative architecture in Spain.

1225 "Sumer is icumen in, Lude sing cucu" is sung as a round in England.

1285 Smog affects London when soft coal is used for heating and cooking; in 1306, a man will be executed for burning coal in the city.

exactly what the separate voices should sing. What's more, they could invent entirely new melodies, not just rely on the plainchants everybody knew. These were the first real composers.

Among them was *HILDEGARD* of Bingen (1098–1179), a visionary poet who also wrote many monophonic melodies; and a little later a group centered on the cathedral of Notre Dame in Paris, including *LÉONIN* (c.1135–1201) and *PÉROTIN* (c.1160–c.1205). The Notre Dame composers wrote organum for two, three, and even four voices, but in a more elaborate style.

The Motet

As well as the plainchants and organum associated with the mass, a new form of sacred composition evolved in the thirteenth century, the motet. This was a three-part form, based on a tenor plainsong melody, with the addition of two original melodies to different texts—a very complex and sophisticated business. The motet caught on in a big way, and soon became a popular secular form too.

This new form of organum still used the plainsong tenor line as a starting point, but slowed it right down and added a completely new, complementary melody (or even two or three melodies) with a free-flowing rhythm. This was the real break with the monophony of the early medieval church, when individual lines of music gained their independence and two or more melodies could be sung simultaneously: polyphony was here to stay.

The men didn't have it all their own way—convents also had choirs, and even composers, such as Hildegard of Bingen.

Women Composers

Interesting: the first composer I mention—Hildegard of Bingen—is a woman. She lived in a misogynist society, too. Not that things have improved much; dozens of good composers are still overlooked because of their gender. For instance there's Clara Schumann (better than her husband Robert, some say), the redoubtable Dame Ethel Smyth, Germaine Tailleferre, and a couple of my favorites, Ruth Crawford Seeger and Elisabeth Lutyens—ooh, and Elizabeth Maconchy. Not forgetting Betsy Jolas, Odaline de la Martinez, and Judith Weir, and . . . well, I'm sure you get the picture.

1300 French medical professor Arnaldus de Villa distills brandy at Montpellier—for medicinal use only, of course.

1322 Bitter oranges—the only kind known in Europe—are traded at the French Mediterranean town of Nice.

1322 Pope John XXII forbids the use of counterpoint in church music.

1300~1350

Ars Nova
Fourteenth-Century France

The history of music is littered with phrases including the word "new" in one language or another, as composers and theorists discarded the conventions of their day and promoted exciting modern styles, which in turn would be superseded by later fashions. So, what you've just got used to thinking of as new, the organum of the thirteenth century, is about to become "Ars Antiqua" in the eyes of the proponents of the ultrahip "Ars Nova."

The term *Ars Nova* (new art) was coined by the French composer *Philippe de Vitry* (1291–1361) as the title for a treatise that described the principles of the new style in detail. One of the major developments was in the sophisticated rhythmic patterns that were used, particularly in the motets, including a device

A monk egging on the boys in the band, and probably picking up a few tips too. Hieronymous Bosch satirizes musicians.

known as isorhythm: a recurrent rhythmic pattern underlying a melody (also recurrent) with a different number of notes, so that the two get out of sync—a really jazzy effect.

> ### " ☆ "
> #### Clever Stuff
>
> What's most striking about the Ars Nova is its complexity. Machaut in particular enjoyed writing ingeniously constructed isorhythms and canons (a bit like rounds, where the voices come in one after another imitatively). He even managed in one *rondeau, Ma fin est mon commencement*, to write lines which read the same backward and forward to match the sense of the text. Now that's smart.

1340 Florentine bankers finance Edward III's war with France; when the latter repudiates his debts, Florentine banks collapse.

1347 Jane I, countess of Provence, attempts to reduce venereal disease in Avignon by arranging for prostitutes to be regularly examined.

1348 Jews become scapegoats and are blamed for spreading the Black Death; atrocities occur in Switzerland and Germany.

Cantus Firmus

As we've seen, the motet started as an elaboration of plainsong melodies. Freely composed tunes were added over a slow-moving tenor line, which was called the *cantus firmus* (fixed song). At first, the words were always sacred texts in Latin, but gradually the *cantus firmus* became the base for secular songs, and by the end of the fourteenth century composers were using popular tunes (a particular favorite was *L'homme armé*) as the *cantus firmus* for their sacred motets, and even during the mass.

Minstrels were often very talented musicians, but some were just show-offs.

Another feature of the Ars Nova was its acceptance of secular texts and tunes. Attitudes in the church were beginning to relax toward profane music: an academy for troubadours (still in existence, now called *Académie des Jeux Floreaux*) was founded in Toulouse in 1323, some measure of the respectability they now enjoyed. De Vitry was a churchman and eventually became Bishop of Meaux, but he also knew quite a lot about the music of the *trouvères* and troubadours.

And this was part of a two-way process. *Trouvères* such as *Adam DE LA HALLE* (c.1245–c.1288) had adapted the sacred motet to secular texts in the vernacular, and if the minstrels could hijack the motet, then why shouldn't the church steal a few ideas from them?

MACHAUT

Outstanding among fourteenth-century French composers was *Guillaume DE MACHAUT* (c.1300–1377), who was just as happy writing love songs as church music:

he wrote both sacred and secular motets, as well as *chansons, rondeaux,* and *virelais*. What's more, he was a distinguished poet as well as a musician—a medieval triple threat. His four-part *Messe de Nostre Dame,* the first surviving polyphonic mass, is well worth listening to. It's a brilliant example of the Ars Nova style, especially in its exciting use of rhythms and intricately interweaving melodic lines, and was to set the standard for polyphonic composition for several generations.

1350s The Black Death, a plague first encountered in Europe in 1348, spreads over the next 20 years, killing about 75 million people (a third to a half of the population).

1368 Nearly a million laborers are conscripted to construct 4,000 miles of the Great Wall of China to defend territory under Ming dynasty domination.

1371 Caxton prints a translation of a French book of travels, by Sir John Mandeville, which has descriptions of fabulous creatures like the Skiapod.

1350~1500

Polyphony Spreads like the Plague
Ars Nova in the Rest of Europe

The effect of the Ars Nova was electrifying. This was music like nothing anybody had heard before: expressive, complex, worldly, and exciting. It captured the mood of the age, when the boundaries between church and secular life were becoming fuzzy, religious dogmatism and symbolism were being replaced by humanist values, and the medieval period was drawing to a close. Polyphony, which had originated in France, became the predominant musical style of a new age, which had its roots in Italy—the Renaissance.

The Renaissance was very expressive of the human condition.

What Exactly Was the Renaissance?
Literally "rebirth," although it wasn't so much a birth as a slow evolution from the church-dominated Middle Ages to a more human-centered, rational society. The movement began in Italy in the fourteenth century, and is generally thought of as lasting until the early seventeenth—but it's impossible to be precise. Renaissance music, however, is generally considered to have begun with the Ars Nova and finished around 1600. Okay?

One of the first composers outside France to catch on to the new music was *Francesco LANDINI* (c.1325–1397), whose music (mainly a type of dance-song called a *ballata*) incorporated the intricacies of the Ars Nova into the harmonious Italian style. There was also interest in polyphony in England—one of the earliest six-part polyphonic pieces was the anonymous "Sumer is icumen in," written in about 1225—and English composers developed French innovations into a distinctive sweet style typified by the music of *John DUNSTABLE* (c.1390–1453).

c.1400 Italian scholars develop a script based on Roman inscriptional capitals and Carolingian small letters— the basis of "Roman" lettering.

1454 "Four and twenty blackbirds baked in a pie" commemorates Philippe Le Bon's Feast of the Pheasant, when 28 musicians perform inside an enormous pie.

1477 Edward IV bans cricket in England because it interferes with the compulsory practice of archery.

TO WATCH

More performers are taking an interest in medieval and Renaissance music than ever before, so there's plenty to listen to. Try to catch some of Dufay's religious works, especially the masses *Se la face ay pale* and *L'Homme armé*, Ockeghem's *Missa "Mi-mi"* and *Missa prolationum*, and just about anything by Josquin—he wrote dozens of motets and *chansons*, and 18 masses, all wonderful stuff.

WORKS

A Renaissance garden party being entertained by a few popular *chansons* of the time.

THE FRANCO-FLEMISH SCHOOL

A center for the new music grew at the court of Burgundy, where artists and musicians flocked to work under the patronage of Duke Philip the Good. Here, *Guillaume DUFAY* (c.1397–1474) bridged the gap between the medieval music of his native France and the sensuous sounds he heard on his travels in Italy, and became the father-figure of Renaissance music. As well as a huge number of *chansons* and motets, he wrote eight masses, one of which deserves special mention: the mass *Se la face ay pale*. This uses as its *cantus firmus* not the plainsong associated with the mass, but a secular *chanson* of the same name that he had written some years before—symbolic of the humanist ideas underlying Renaissance thinking.

A contemporary of Dufay in Burgundy was the Franco-Fleming *GILLES DE BINS*, known as *BINCHOIS* (c.1400–1460), whose secular *chansons* were as popular as Dufay's religious works. Their music was an inspiration to the next generation of Franco-Flemish composers, such as *Johannes OCKEGHEM* (c.1410–c.1497) and the Frenchman *Josquin DES PRÉZ* (c.1440–1521)—usually known simply as Josquin—who was the most gifted and individual composer of the early Renaissance. He wrote over eighteen complete masses, including several based on popular tunes, and numerous motets (not unlike masses, but smaller scale) and secular songs.

The Organ

Not only did the church embrace secular styles in this period, it also relaxed its ban on musical instruments. Although a lot of sacred music was still for unaccompanied voices, one instrument was beginning to find favor with masses—the organ. Both portable organs ("portatives") originally used by minstrels, and larger, built-in organs soon became specifically associated with church music.

| **1501** In Venice, music is printed for the first time using movable type. | **1501** Vasco da Gama cuts off the trade route through Egypt to Alexandria and wins control of the spice trade for Lisbon. | **1508-12** Michelangelo paints the ceiling frescoes of the Sistine chapel. |  | **1517** Martin Luther nails his 95 theses to a castle door in Wittenberg, marking the beginning of the Reformation. |

1500~1600

The Italian Job
The High Renaissance

Back in Italy, the Renaissance was really flourishing. As the Franco-Flemish School reached its peak with the music of Josquin, the Italian style was beginning to gain in popularity, and musical attention moved from the north to the cities of Italy. One of the reasons for this was the Reformation taking place in Northern Europe (more on that later), and the backlash in Catholicism known as the Counter-Reformation. In a nutshell, the effect of both these movements was to force simplicity onto church music—which suited the Italian style, with its sweet-sounding and relatively uncomplicated imitative polyphony, better than the Franco-Flemish.

Giovanni Pierluigi da Palestrina musing over yet another masterpiece.

Music Publishing

Let us now pay homage to Ottaviano Petrucci, one of the unsung heroes of musical history. His contribution was the development of a method of printing music, creating an explosion in the availability of new music. The first book of vocal pieces hit the streets of Venice in 1501, and by the middle of the century music was rolling off the presses all over Europe.

The two great composers of the High Renaissance are the Italian *Giovanni DA PALESTRINA* (1525–94) and *Orlando di LASSUS* (1532–94), a Franco-Fleming who spent his early life in Italy. Palestrina was *maestro di cappella* (musical director) of several churches in Rome, and was a prolific composer of church music. He wrote almost 400 motets and over 100 masses, some based on a *cantus firmus*, others freely composed. On top of this long list of works, he wrote a fair number of madrigals (polyphonic settings of poetry), all rather conservative in style, but despite that they are gorgeously well crafted. Lasso, who was similarly prolific, was

1550 Billiards is played for the first time in Italy.

1587 The regent of Japan commissions a vast statue of the Buddha; all civilians are required to contribute their swords and guns for its construction.

rather more adventurous, especially in his motets, achieving a truly cosmopolitan style combining a lushness that is typical of the Italians with the rigor associated with the Germanic. After working in Naples, Florence, Rome, and Antwerp, he became *maestro di cappella* at the court of Bavaria.

" ☆ "

A Colorful Character

Don Carlo Gesualdo (c.1560–1613), prince of Venosa, wrote mainly vocal pieces, which are remarkable for their expressive, discordant harmonies and abrupt changes of mood. Not surprising really, since that's the kind of guy he was—he spent much of his life in a deep melancholy, and notoriously had his wife and her lover murdered. But don't let that put you off, his music is weirdly wonderful.

NAMES TO NOTE

Another Italian to look out for is **Luca Marenzio** *(c.1553–1599), and two expatriate Flemings in Italy:* **Adrian Willaert** *(c.1490–1562) and* **Jacob Arcadelt** *(c.1505–1568). Their compatriot,* **Jacobus Clemens non Papa** *(c.1510–c.1556) is also worth mentioning, as is an Italian who spent some time in England,* **Alfonso Ferrabosco** *(1543–88). And don't miss* **John Taverner** *(c.1490–1545) or* **Thomas Tallis** *(c.1505–1585), whose 40-part* Spem in alium *is really something.*

ELSEWHERE . . .

Tomás Luis DE VICTORIA (1548–1611) spent his formative years in Rome, before returning to his native Spain. His music is similar to Palestrina's in approach, but more dramatic, and has the religious fervor we might expect from the land of the Inquisition and Ignatius Loyola.

For composers who never made it to Italy, there was now a thriving music publishing business that brought new music to them. One such was *William* BYRD (1543–1623), who wrote Roman Catholic music, including three stunning masses, despite living in Protestant England.

But the High Renaissance really took off in Venice, where *Andrea* GABRIELI (c.1510–1585) and later his nephew Giovanni, were developing a new sound—and ushering in a new era . . .

Orlando di Lassus poses with the musicians of the Bavarian court. Lassus won the church's ear with his cosmopolitan compositions.

| **1431** Philippe le Bon founds the Chapelle de Bourgogne in Brussels; it will become one of the most famous centers for music in Europe. | **c.1440** The first Gypsies begin to arrive in Spain; they will maintain Andalusian Moorish traditions in song and dance in Spain after the Moors are expelled. | **1500** *Till Eulenspiegel* appears, a collection of stories about the farcical antics of Till, a shrewd peasant trickster who gets the better of city folk. | **1508** Leonardo da Vinci describes the principle of fitting an artificial lens to the surface of the eye. |

1400~1600

Let's Dance

Instrumental Music

A singer, flautist, and lutenist. Domestic music-making was a suitable pastime for young ladies.

It took a long time for Europe to shake off the notion that musical instruments were inherently sinful, and they were only grudgingly accepted for accompanying vocal music during the Middle Ages— except among the minstrels and peasants, of course, who indulged in such vices as dancing. But attitudes changed radically in the Renaissance, giving purely instrumental music (essentially a secular genre) some respectability, and laying the foundations for modern concert music.

By about 1400, noblemen were employing minstrels on a more permanent basis, and the medieval wandering minstrels had evolved into Renaissance court musicians. Just about every prince, duke, and even some towns had a band, which was expected to provide music for social and ceremonial occasions. There were loud bands for outdoor functions, using wind instruments such as cornetts (strident instruments that looked like bent recorders but sounded more like trumpets), sackbuts (early trombones), shawms (early oboes), pipes, and drums. And there were quieter "consorts" of recorders or viols (predecessors of the violin family) for more refined indoor events.

Early Music

Recently there's been a surge of interest in what is loosely called "early music" (written before about 1650), which has given a lot of previously unknown pieces an airing. There's also a movement toward "authentic performance"—performing as nearly as possible in the original manner, using period instruments. Opinions are divided as to the value of "authenticity," but it has produced some remarkable performances.

1515–17 An overzealous Dominican friar makes a record-breaking tour selling "indulgences"; German ecclesiastical credit collapses, precipitating the Reformation.

1561 Jean Nicot, French ambassador to Lisbon, sends tobacco seeds and leaves to the queen mother, Catherine de Medici; nicotine enshrines his name.

" ☆ "

Weird and Wonderful Instruments

Renaissance instrument-makers had a penchant for odd shapes. The viol and recorder families were disappointingly conventional, but the wind instruments were something else—ranging from the crumhorn (a sort of musical walking stick) and the racket (a bass tobacco jar), to the cornett and the serpent (imagine a python with rigor mortis).

These bands were phenomenally popular, and even "serious" composers started to write for them. Most of the pieces they played were arrangements of vocal music, but what really caught the public's attention were the dances: estampies, pavanes, galliards, passamezzos, saltarellos, and many more. They were often grouped together as "dance suites," a form that was the ancestor of the symphony.

GOING SOLO

The increasing popularity and availability (thanks to music printing) of instrumental music coincided with the growth of an educated middle class. Singing and playing music was considered a necessary social grace, and the public needed music that they could play themselves. Composers jumped on the bandwagon by writing pieces that could be performed by amateurs as well as professionals.

As well as consort music for all sorts of combinations of instruments—"whole" consorts, comprising instruments of one family, such as recorders or viols; and

"broken" consorts combining string and wind instruments—and the ubiquitous songs and madrigals, there was a growing market for solo instrumental pieces for the lute, or for the various keyboard instruments that were around: spinets, virginals, clavichords, and harpsichords (see pp. 58–59).

Often these pieces were keyboard arrangements of popular songs (a trend that continues today), but new forms such as the fantasia (or fancy), theme and variations, and canzona developed to show off the capabilities of these instruments.

Gentry enjoy the latest dance craze at a Renaissance ball.

The Lute

The instrument we now associate most closely with the Renaissance, the lute, had actually been around for ages, and is by no means exclusively European. Versions of the lute appear in most musical cultures worldwide, many being descendants of an Arabic instrument, *al-'ud* (from which we get the word "lute"). The name arrived in the West via Moorish Spain, which was greatly influenced by the Arab world.

1565 Pencils are manufactured in England for the first time.

1592 The remains of Pompeii are discovered in the course of work on an underground water line.

1600 Will Kemp, dancer and comedian, does a Morris dance all the way from London to Norwich; he records this in *Kemp's Nine Daies Wonder*.

1550~1650

Gloriana
England's Golden Age

Elizabethan England lapped up all the Italian music it could get its hands on, and collections such as Musica Transalpina *(1588) were bestsellers. With Good Queen Bess on the throne, England was prospering, and the exciting Mediterranean style was an inspiration to young composers. The emphasis was on self-expression, and there was an explosion of madrigals, consorts, lute songs, and instrumental pieces in a distinctly English style.*

Weelkes's Disastrous Career

Thomas Weelkes, madrigalist *par excellence*, maybe chose a career path not entirely suited to his talents. His appointments as organist and choirmaster at Winchester College and later at Chichester Cathedral didn't quite square up with his prodigious appetite for alcohol, leading to his eventual dismissal for, so the story goes, urinating on the Dean from the organ loft.

Elizabeth I, whose reign was the golden age of English madrigals and consorts.

The growth industry was composing music for amateurs to perform at home. Anybody who aspired to being part of society was expected to either sing or play an instrument, and the well-to-do got together for evenings of madrigals or consort music. Printed music, often set out ingeniously on large sheets that could be read by performers sitting around a table, sold like hot cakes.

This was the age of Shakespeare, there was a wealth of good poetry around, and the most popular vocal music was the madrigal. Literally dozens of composers wrote madrigals and similar part-songs, but a few great madrigalists stood out: *Thomas MORLEY* (c.1557–1602), *John WILBYE* (1574–1638), and *Thomas WEELKES* (1576–1623). Their work showed a huge emotional breadth, usually expressing either the joys or sorrows of romantic love, together with great stylistic fluency.

One of the tricks they picked up from the Italians was "word-painting":

1605 Catholic conspirators plan to overthrow the Protestant monarchy in Britain by blowing up the English Parliament, but the "Gunpowder Plot" is discovered.

1648 English music publisher John Playford establishes himself in London; he will have a virtual monopoly on music publishing until his death.

1657 A 12-year-old boy from Shepton Mallet in Somerset is "bewitched" and is observed to fly 30 yards over a garden wall.

The Madrigal

You may be wondering what a madrigal actually is. Basically, it's a setting of poetry for between three and six voices. It originated in Italy, where it was taken very seriously. But the English madrigal, although sometimes just as serious, tended to be more lighthearted, with catchy rhythms and risqué *double entendres*. A related form was the ballett, which had a dancelike feel and often a fa-la-la or hey-nonny-no refrain.

illustrating individual words or phrases with an appropriate musical gesture, such as a descending phrase on the word "down," or a harsh discord on the word "pain." Examples can be found in many madrigals, but try Wilbye's *Sweet hony sucking bees*, or Weelkes's extraordinary *Thule, the period of cosmography* and *O care thou wilt despatch mee*, and you'll see what I mean.

Instrumental music was flourishing too. As well as the inevitable arrangements of madrigals, original compositions for lute, keyboard, and consorts of all kinds were being created. It looked like a good time was being had by all.

Well, not quite all . . . *John DOWLAND* (1563–1626), possibly the finest composer of the period, made his name by being melancholy. He reached superstar status in his day, but was an incurable depressive. Few of his numerous lute songs, consorts, and vocal pieces showed a glimmer of cheerfulness—a perfect foil for all the fa-la-las. Don't miss the *Lachrimae* for viols, *Semper dolens, semper Dowland*, or such songs as *In darkness let me dwell* or *Weep you no more sad fountains*. Be prepared—they're real tearjerkers!

Something of a party— English musicians get together for an evening of consort music.

1597 Japan's government, convinced that the activities of Christian missionaries will lead to colonization by European powers, banishes them.

1600 The urban population of Europe is 5 percent of the total; in the Netherlands it is 15 percent.

1601 An East India Company captain doses his crew with lemon juice, protecting them from scurvy; almost 200 years later, the Royal Navy will follow suit.

1607 English vagrants protest against the enclosure of common lands and other abuses by the landed gentry; several are killed and three are hanged.

1550~1650
Birth in Venice
Dynamic Stereo!

Galileo and Milton discussing the burning issues of the day.

The city-state of Venice was the trading and cultural center of Europe, and epitomized the spirit of the age: boundaries between sacred and secular, church and state, nobleman and peasant, were blurred. The head of state, the doge, was elected rather than born to the job, and he presided over both the spiritual and political affairs of the city. Much of the ceremony that attached to the job took place in the basilica of St. Mark or nearby, and music played an important role in these public functions.

And what gorgeous music it was! *Andrea Gabrieli* (1510–85) hit upon the idea of combining choirs with groups of instruments (cornetts and sackbuts), producing a sumptuous sound that matched the opulence of the time perfectly. Placing more emphasis on the richness of the harmonies than the interplay of the different voices, he simplified the

polyphonic style, giving the music a sense of grandeur. Most dramatically, though, he experimented with the spatial possibilities of St. Mark's, using a device called antiphony: placing different groups of

🗨️ "⭐" Science versus Religion

Outside Venice, the church wasn't quite as tolerant of new ideas yet. Science contradicted traditional teachings, and people like poor old Galileo Galilei were hauled up in front of the Inquisition for their "heresies." Nevertheless, although the simplification of polyphony smacked of humanism, it did make the services more accessible to the layman…

1618 Astronomer Johannes Kepler discovers the law of planetary motion, making it possible to calculate the distance between Earth and the sun.

1625 The goiter, when only moderately swollen, is esteemed a mark of beauty; Peter Paul Rubens's portrait of Marie de Medici does not disguise this deformity.

performers in various places around the church to give a stereo (or even quadra) effect.

His nephew *Giovanni GABRIELI* (c.1554–1612) carried on the family tradition and published music by both of them, including canzonas (ensemble pieces in the new style) and sonatas (pieces to be played, as opposed to cantatas, pieces to be sung), and also a new

Claudio Monteverdi offers us music in the new Baroque style.

form, which he called concerti. These instrumental works, with contrasting groups of instruments (for example, strings and brass) holding a kind of dialogue, were the ancestors of the modern concerto, which contrasts a solo instrument with the full orchestra.

St. Mark's

One of the reasons antiphony caught on in Venice was the architecture of St. Mark's. Its huge interior was suited better acoustically to chordal than polyphonic music, and included various ideal places for choirs and instrumental ensembles. Music came to the audience from all directions—organ galleries, balconies, and platforms around the altar area—and the effect was devastatingly magnificent.

GOOD-BYE RENAISSANCE, HELLO BAROQUE

The emphasis on contrast and harmony, rather than polyphony, marked the end of the Renaissance period in music, and foreshadowed the next era—the Baroque. The composer who bridged the gap between Renaissance and Baroque music, *Claudio MONTEVERDI* (1567–1643), ended up in Venice as *maestro di capella* at St. Mark's, following in the footsteps of the Gabrielis. But the century started with a literally dramatic development—opera.

A procession in St. Mark's Square, Venice, accompanied by wind band.

Piano and Forte

The juxtaposition of loud and soft instruments was a feature of both Gabrielis' music, but young Giovanni really showed it to its best advantage. His *Sonata pian' e forte* not only has opposing "choirs" of brass instruments and a single viol, but also specifies when they should play softly or loudly (*piano* or *forte*). Revolutionary stuff, and still breathtaking 400 years later.

1600 An inventory of Elizabeth I's wardrobe, excluding robes for state occasions, includes102 French gowns, 99 robes, 100 loose gowns, and 125 petticoats.

1600 The population of the Americas is probably half what it was in 1500, due largely to European microbes, particularly smallpox.

1605 Spanish novelist, playwright, and poet Miguel de Cervantes's *Don Quixote*, initially conceived as a satire on the novel of chivalry, will be considered a world masterpiece.

1550~1650

The Fat Lady Sings

The Emergence of Opera

The harpsichord and cello continuo gave a chordal basis to Baroque music.

While the Gabrielis were doing their thing for choral and instrumental music in Venice, a bunch of intellectuals in Florence calling themselves the Camerata were debating the big issues of the day. There were a few musicians among them, including Jacopo PERI (1561–1633) and Giulio CACCINI (c.1548–1618), and one of the things under discussion was whether the music or the words were more important in vocal music. In polyphonic music it's almost impossible to follow the words, and the Camerata were looking for a way to resolve the problem.

At that time there was a craze for anything classical (i.e., Greco-Roman), so they suggested copying what they imagined was the Ancient Greek style—a single melodic line with simple accompaniment. This idea, though hardly new, was revolutionary. Monody, as the style was called, meant that the words could be heard clearly—allowing composers to set texts that told a story. Pretty soon another of the Camerata's dreams was to come true: a re-creation of Greek-style drama set to music. Opera arrived in 1597 with a production of Peri's *Dafne* (sadly lost), which got the ball rolling—and Monteverdi picked it up and ran with it.

I'm not going to dwell too much on the subject (see the excellent Crash Course in opera!), but some of the features of early opera were to affect all music, and set the tone for the Baroque period.

Continuo

Music of the early seventeenth century was often simply a melody with a chordal accompaniment—usually played by a bass instrument such as a cello or viol, together with a keyboard instrument such as a harpsichord or organ. This accompaniment was written in a sort of musical shorthand known as the *basso continuo* (or just *continuo* for short), and became a ubiquitous feature of Baroque music.

1607 Captain John Smith, attempting to trade for corn with the Algonquins, is captured. The Powhatan chief's 12-year-old daughter Pocahontas saves his life.

1635 French painter Abraham Bossé, in his series *The Five Senses,* chooses an artichoke to embody Taste.

1679 Johann Wolfgang Franck writes *Die Drey Tochter Cecrops,* the earliest extant example of a German opera.

TO WATCH

WORKS

The first operas were like the first pancake—not as good as the next. Monteverdi was the first to master the genre, and it's worth trying *Orfeo* and *L'incoronazione di Poppea.* His nonoperatic works deserve a hearing too, especially the *Vespers* of 1610, which show a kaleidoscopic mixture of old and new styles, and his large and varied output of madrigals. Another composer to look out for is Caccini, who published a book of monodic vocal music called *Le nuove musiche.*

TO WATCH

WORKS

The most noticeable innovation was the use of recitative, a rhythmically free declamation with a simple chordal accompaniment, in which singers could fill in the plot between more strictly formal songs, the arias. This alternation of recitative and aria was also used in the cantata, a sort of unstaged opera that emerged in the seventeenth century.

Other more general elements were evident too, which became trademarks of the Baroque style. Monody placed the emphasis on a single melodic line, which could be embellished with all sorts of ornaments, and allowed more intricate rhythms to stand out: the melody was supported by a chordal accompaniment, in which harmony was more important than polyphony; and contrast of all sorts—loud and soft, fast and slow, large and small groups—replaced the homogeneity of Renaissance music.

WHY ARE SO MANY MUSICAL TERMS IN ITALIAN?

Simple really—the first instructions as to how a piece should be played appeared in Italian music. Until the late 1500s, nobody specified whether a piece was loud or soft, or what speed the thing should go—performers were expected to know all that. The Italians did it first, and the practice has, generally speaking, stuck.

The first operas, such as Monteverdi's *L'incoronazione di Poppea,* were often based on myth and legend.

Digression

Getting It Together

Let's take a break from history again and look a bit more closely at some of the theory. We've already seen how the notes are written down; now it's time to see how music is composed from the raw materials of rhythm, melody, harmony, etc., and what those terms actually mean.

The different voices in a choir combine together in rich harmony, or complex counterpoint.

RHYTHM

Most music is divided into bite-sized chunks known as bars, which define the underlying beat of the piece. A waltz, for example, has three beats in each bar, and the first beat of each bar is accented—*one*, two, three, *one*, two, three, etc. Similarly, a march (*left*, right, *left*, right) has two beats to the bar, and a huge number of pieces have four. The time signature at the beginning of a piece (see example 1) shows the number of beats (the upper number), and what kind of beat (the lower number)—for example, 3/4 indicates three quarter note beats to the bar. The speed of this basic beat, the tempo, is shown by instructions such as *allegro* (fast) or *lento* (slow), or by a metronome marking (see example 1), which specifies how many beats per minute. Having fixed a tempo and a beat, a composer can create different rhythms by using notes of various lengths to subdivide the bar—and the permutations are endless.

♩ = 80 *Metronome marking*

EXAMPLE 1

Time signature

A simple melody, harmonized with three-part chords.

Triad (C Major)

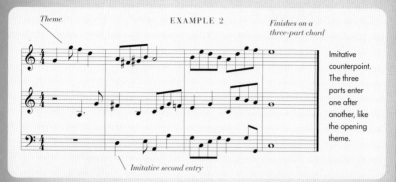

Theme

EXAMPLE 2

Finishes on a three-part chord

Imitative counterpoint. The three parts enter one after another, like the opening theme.

Imitative second entry

MELODY

Rhythm alone doesn't make for a good tune—without some change of pitch it's literally monotonous. One can argue about the definition of "melody," but let's say that it's a succession of notes that form an interesting line. Some melodies are smooth and progress in small steps (like the top line in example 1), others are angular, jumping larger intervals between notes (as in example 2).

HARMONY

What we've been talking about so far has been the horizontal placing of notes—one note following another. But if we arrange them vertically, so they sound simultaneously, we have a chord. Any two or more notes played together form a chord, but only

certain combinations harmonize with each other: the interval of an octave (eight notes, from C to C, or A to A, for example) is a concord, but a semitone (the smallest interval, such as E to F, or C to C sharp) forms a dissonance. Most classical harmony is based on the intervals of thirds (three notes apart, such as C to E, and E to G) and fifths (C to G, or A to E—get the idea?), to form three-part chords called triads.

COUNTERPOINT

If we combine the idea of horizontal melody with vertical harmony, we eventually reach counterpoint —the superimposition of two or more melodic lines. Each line has its own tune, but they also blend together so that on the strong beats of the bar they form harmonies (see example 2). Clever stuff.

A young violinist picks out a melody.

1597 Images of flowers and fruit from *Gerard's Herbal* are copied for embroidery, popular among the merchant class of England.

1602 Galileo discovers the laws of gravitation and oscillation.

1625 Neapolitans live well, buying in what they cannot produce; this year alone, they import 1,500 tons of sugar and 500 tons of honey.

1600~1650

Overture and Beginners, Please
Italy

Opera was to dominate the music scene in Italy from this period onward, and to have a strong influence on other forms too. As composers got to feel more at home in the genre, they used the lilting speech patterns of the rich Italian language to shape their style, and the growing number of virtuoso operatic soloists on the scene encouraged them to write more flamboyant arias. The resulting lyrical and elaborate style became known as bel canto *(beautiful singing).*

Opera soon became a multimedia event, combining music with drama and creating the *prima donna*.

Foremost among these composers were *Pietro Francesco Cavalli* (1602–76) and *Antonio Cesti* (1623–69), both of whom wrote exclusively vocal music, including operas, in the monodic style. While Monteverdi had striven to achieve dramatic contrast and forceful expression, his successors aimed for a more graceful, singable style, and were unashamedly populist. Their operas were written for those who wanted melodies and to hear soloists showing off; these are the origins of a style that has made opera performances in Italy as popular as soccer matches.

Opera was still centered in Venice, but its influence was already being felt all over Italy. In Rome, center of the Catholic church, *Giacomo Carissimi* (1605–74) was applying some of the techniques of the new

Oratorio

A sort of cousin to opera, oratorio developed at much the same time. Like opera, it has arias, recitatives, and choruses, with orchestral accompaniment, and sets a story to music. So what's the difference? Well, first it's not acted out theatrically like opera, but more importantly it's a setting of a sacred text, usually taken from the Bible. Actually, musically there's very little difference.

1625 *La Liberazione di Ruggiero dall'Isola d'Alcina* is the first opera written by a woman, Francesca Cannini; Handel will write his opera *Alcina* in 1734.

1628 Gianlorenzo Bernini, the most important artist of the Italian Baroque, begins the tomb of Urban VIII.

1641 All foreigners have been expelled from Japan except the Dutch; they are allowed to leave their small island in Nagasaki harbor only once a year.

style to sacred music. As well as a number of masses and motets, Carissimi wrote several oratorios, settings of sacred texts, which were similar in style and dramatic impact to Monteverdi's operas. These not only had recitatives and arias, but also used choruses rather like a Greek chorus, to comment on the story or help the narrative.

THE BOYS IN THE BAND

But opera wasn't just influencing vocal music. There were often instrumental interludes and dances incorporated into the action—and, to cover the noise of latecomers, an overture. The accompanying band of instruments was expanding to become a true orchestra, and specific forms were evolving for the new ensembles: the instrumental sonata developed from the dance suite, the concerto from the antiphonal pieces by the Gabrielis, and the

> **" ☆ "**
>
> ### A Cut Above the Rest
>
> Some singers gave up more than just the day job. A simple operation could preserve a boy's unbroken treble voice, enabling him to carry on singing the high lines so popular in Baroque opera. A good castrato could earn colossal fees, and several reached superstar status—presumably they thought it worth the sacrifice.

near-contemporary of Monteverdi, *Girolamo FRESCOBALDI* (1583–1643), composed much vocal music, but is remembered mainly for his pieces for organ and harpsichord, which, it has been said, he played with brilliant virtuosity.

Frescobaldi adopted the dramatic harmonic style of Monteverdi in his music, but was also capable of complex counterpoint and elaborately ornamented melodic lines that became a feature of Baroque keyboard music.

Frescobaldi was a wizard at the keyboard, and created a new style of harpsichord composition.

overture tended to follow a conventional fast-slow-fast pattern, which evolved to become the foundation of the symphony.

Solo instrumental music was thriving too—especially for the keyboard. A

WORKS TO WATCH

To get some idea of the early *bel canto* style, try Cavalli's *Didone, Ormindo,* or *Calisto,* and Cesti's comic opera *Il pomo d'oro* (great title—it translates as "The tomato"); and as an introduction to oratorio, Carissimi's *Jephte* or *Baltazar.* Another piece of the same period, but totally different in style, is *Miserere* by Gregorio Allegri (1585–1629)—simple, but gorgeous.

WORKS TO WATCH

c.1600 Developed in Central American colonies and further refined in Spain, the zarabanda, chacona, pasacalle, and folia dances become popular in Europe.

1618 Bohemian Protestants revolt against the Counter-Reformation, and the Thirty Years' War begins.

1626 Sir Francis Bacon attempts to freeze chickens by stuffing them with snow. He catches pneumonia and dies.

1600~1650

The Okay Chorale
Germany and the Netherlands

In the north, the transition from Renaissance to Baroque was less dramatic than in Italy. The Germanic temperament was not entirely comfortable with the extrovert character of Italian music, and a more staid approach developed in the Netherlands and Germany. Besides, since the Reformation, northern Europe was predominantly Protestant, and had a rather puritanical attitude toward secular music.

Church and Court

From the seventeenth century until well into the nineteenth, musicians had a choice of two employers—either the church or one of the aristocratic courts. Although music publishing was well established, it wasn't a moneymaking business, and freelance musicians were unheard of. The only way to survive financially was to get a job with a patron, providing him or her with music on demand.

Johann Schein was one of the foremost composers in the seventeenth century, but had his bad-hair days.

Yet music still played an important part in worship in the reformed church. Gone were the plainchants with Latin texts, but *Martin LUTHER* (1483–1546) had replaced them with German texts set to more user-friendly hymn tunes (some of

which he composed himself), called *chorales*, which then came to be used as the basis for new compositions.

Samuel SCHEIDT (1586–1630) and *Johann Hermann SCHEIN* (1587–1654) successfully combined Lutheran chorales with elements of the new Italian style; the outcome was a distinctly Germanic Baroque sound. Their contemporary *Heinrich SCHÜTZ* (1585–1672), who had studied in Venice with Giovanni Gabrieli, proved himself to be even more open to new Italian ideas. This can be heard especially in his earlier music. His output was almost exclusively vocal, and ranges from rather conservative polyphonic motets through Italianate choral works to the somber Germanic oratorios and passions of his later years.

1634 Thomas Prys, soldier, pirate, landowner, and poet, dies; in his most moving poem, he exhorts his cousin and heir to abandon piracy.

1643 John Milton's *The Doctrine and Discipline of Divorce* argues that those who live chastely are more likely to make unhappy marriages than those who do not.

1645 Heinrich Schütz's *Seven Words from the Cross* uses four *viole da gamba* to accompany Christ's words, anticipating Bach's *St. Matthew Passion*.

Schein and Scheidt both wrote instrumental as well as vocal music. To some extent Scheidt, who wrote organ and harpsichord music, followed in the footsteps of the Netherlander *Jan Pieterszoon SWEELINCK* (1562–1621), who had established a tradition of keyboard composition similar in style to the English harpsichord composers: but Schein was more an organist than harpsichordist, and his keyboard works are often based on chorale tunes—a device used in German organ music throughout the Baroque period.

And there was a lot of German Baroque organ music in the Baroque. The giant among seventeenth-century exponents of the genre was undoubtedly *Dietrich BUXTEHUDE* (c.1637–1707), a Dane who moved to Germany in 1668. He was a prolific composer of all sorts of music, but it is for his organ music that he is best known. There are toccatas (which are freely composed virtuosic showpieces), elaborately worked-out fugues (very strict imitative counter-point), and chorale preludes, which are highly inventive ornamented versions of Lutheran chorale melodies. Buxtehude had enormous influence on other German composers, so it's a shame he's been so overshadowed by the next generation, which included *Johann PACHELBEL* (1653–1706) and, a little later, one J. S. Bach.

Municipal bands show a light side to Baroque music as they serenade their audience.

❝ ☆ ❞

A Dedicated Follower

While Buxtehude was working at St. Mary's, Lübeck, he gave a series of Sunday afternoon concerts known as *Abendmusik* (evening music). They were immensely popular, and one young fan, the 20-year-old J. S. Bach, walked up from Arnstadt to hear him play the organ. He must have been very enthusiastic—it's about 250 miles.

Schütz, who composed the first German opera.

1650 The Ukiyo-e (literally, "pictures of the floating world") school of art begins to flourish in Japan, producing paintings, woodblock prints, and illustrated books.

1651 Richard Ligon describes rum: "a hot, hellish and terrible liquor" made of "suggar canes, distilled" in Barbados.

1661 Louis XIV starts modifying the Palace of Versailles; up to 30,000 workers will be employed on a palace with a façade half a mile long.

1650~1750

The French Connection
Lully Goes to Court

The French were less puritanical than their Protestant neighbors about the new music coming from Italy, and already had a taste for entertainment that welcomed the advent of opera, ballet, and secular instrumental music. The House of Bourbon, especially in the reign of Louis XIV, was a lavish sponsor of the arts, employing some of the finest musicians in Europe. One was a young Italian who became the most influential composer in the country, and the father figure of French opera.

Lully, who reigned supreme over musical life in France.

Jean-Baptiste LULLY (originally Giovanni Battista Lulli) (1632–1687) moved to France at the age of 13, and virtually taught himself music—so he didn't exactly bring Italian opera into France, but can be credited with adapting it to suit the French language and temperament. From his first job as attendant to the king's cousin, he rose through the ranks to become director of the royal orchestra, court composer, and music master to the royal family—all by the

The Palace of Versailles, Louis XIV's little country pad, and Lully's stamping ground (until the accident).

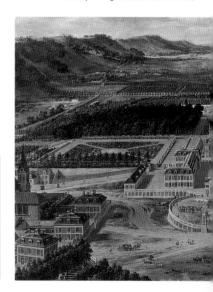

66 ☆ 99

The Dangers of Conducting

As orchestras got bigger, a conductor became necessary to keep time. Lully, director of one of the first real orchestras, became one of the first conductors. He literally beat time, banging a large stick on the floor. Alas, his aim was not always too good. One day he hit his foot, contracted blood poisoning, and died.

age of 30. His main claim to fame lies with his dramatic works, the result of collaborations with writers such as Molière and Quinault. Equally important, though —at least as far as this Crash Course is concerned—was his music for the king's "24 violins," the court orchestra. This was an unusually large collection of instruments for the time, the forerunner of the modern concert orchestra.

TO WATCH WORKS

You can get some idea of the emergent French style from Lully's comic ballet *Le Bourgeois gentilhomme* and the opera *Alceste*. If opera's not your thing, then you'll find there's some delightful keyboard music by both Rameau and Couperin in a very approachable style.

WORKS TO WATCH

Other composers, however, notably *Marc-Antoine CHARPENTIER* (1645–1704), wrote comparatively little opera and concentrated on sacred pieces—possibly because Lully had the monopoly on music for the stage.

In fact, Lully so dominated the French scene that it wasn't until he died that other composers emerged, such as *Jean-Philippe RAMEAU* (1683–1764), who was rather more serious-minded and academic, and a gifted keyboard player. Rameau's operas never achieved the popularity Lully had enjoyed (although in many ways they are better crafted), which was a bitter disappointment to his ambitions, but he gained some respect for his collections of harpsichord music and sonatas in the Italian style.

There were even some composers who didn't bother at all with opera. There was a growing market for solo keyboard music, and *François COUPERIN* (1668–1733), who came from a family of organists and harpsichordists, not only catered for demand with several books of harpsichord pieces, but also wrote a treatise on the art of playing the harpsichord, *L'Art de toucher le clavecin*.

Court in the Act

Louis XIV, the Sun King, didn't do anything by halves. He considered himself absolute monarch, and spared no expense on little luxuries like the Palace of Versailles. The king was so impressed (or flattered) by Lully that he gave him every musical post going, as well as absolute control over all musical drama across the country— and Lully's blatant pederasty was overlooked (although it was a capital offense for everyone else).

1648 The followers of George Fox, an English lay preacher, found the Society of Friends, or Quakers (because of their agitated movements at moments of divine revelation).

1666 The Great Fire begins in Pudding Lane near London Bridge; in four days it will destroy four-fifths of the walled city.

1674 A "Women's Petition against Coffee" published in London complains that men are always in the coffee houses at times of domestic crisis, and that coffee makes them impotent.

1650~1775

Britannia Rules the Staves
The Baroque in England

RIGHT Henry Purcell greatest of the English Baroque composers

Masques were often just an excuse for dressing up.

If Germany accepted the Italian Baroque style rather reluctantly, Britain was almost hostile to it. There were several reasons for this: like Germany, Britain was predominantly Protestant and becoming increasingly Puritan; the English language was not at all suited to the monodic recitative style; and more importantly, the Renaissance style had also come rather late to Britain, and was really flourishing at the turn of the seventeenth century. The madrigals, consorts, and keyboard music of the Elizabethan period were so good—if it ain't broke . . .

Oliver Cromwell

Although we might applaud many of the democratic reforms that Cromwell's Common-wealth instituted, they were a body blow for music in England. Patronage of music by both court and church suddenly disappeared, and the whole country fell silent. Apart from Purcell, it took another 250 years for a truly great English composer to emerge. That's another fine mess you got us into, Ollie.

But the idea of drama with music appealed, even if opera *per se* didn't, and a popular entertainment called "masque" evolved. This was a sort of mixed-media happening, with poetry, dance, songs, and instrumental music, and was just catching on when Cromwell came to power—which rather put the damper on things. Until the restoration of the monarchy, music was discouraged, putting an abrupt end not only to the development of English opera but the golden age of English music in general.

It took quite a while for music to re-establish itself into cultural life. The new king, Charles II, reopened the Chapel Royal—a major musical institution—where two composers started their careers as choirboys. The first was *John BLOW*

With Great Glee...

Although the madrigal was effectively killed off by Cromwell, the tradition of part-songs continued in the Restoration and well into the nineteenth century in the form of glees. These were generally for male voices only, often sung by glee clubs, which met in the more salubrious taverns and coffee houses.

1694 John Dunton's *The Ladies Dictionary* describes a Tour: "an artificial dress of Hair, first invented by some Ladies that had lost their own Hair."

1721 When the "South Sea Bubble" investment scheme bursts, British Chancellor John Aislabie is imprisoned for "infamous corruption."

1728 John Broadwood and Sons, the oldest firm of keyboard-instrument makers still in business, is founded by the Swiss harpsichord-maker Burkhard Tshudi.

PUTTING ON AYRES

He was also a prolific composer of secular vocal music, including odes, ayres, catches, and so on, so it's not surprising that he should write songs and incidental music for the theater, and the first English opera, *Dido and Aeneas*. He should have gone on to establish a truly English operatic style, but his untimely death robbed us of that treat. Other composers tried to follow in his footsteps, notably *Thomas ARNE* (1710–78) (who wrote "Rule Britannia") and *William BOYCE* (1711–79), but now the field was open for an invasion of Italian-style opera, strangely enough led by a German immigrant called Handel.

(1649–1708), whose sacred and keyboard works earned him the job of organist at Westminster Abbey, but he was soon eclipsed by one of his pupils at the Chapel Royal, *Henry PURCELL* (1659–95).

Purcell's earliest music was very much in the mold of Byrd and Gibbons, but he soon showed a startlingly original streak, using the bold contrasts characteristic of the Italian Baroque—but with a rhythmic freedom that echoed the English language. Although he continued to write anthems (the English equivalent of motets) in a rather conservative style, his instrumental music, especially the keyboard pieces, showed his inventiveness and mastery of the genre.

WORKS TO WATCH

As well as *Dido and Aeneas*, Purcell wrote a few "semi-operas" such as *The Fairy Queen* and *King Arthur*, which give an idea of his style. Better, in my opinion, are the odes, especially "Come, ye sons of art" and the "Ode for St. Cecilia's Day," and just about all the instrumental music: don't miss the *Funeral Music for Queen Mary* or the string fantasies.

Arne's patriotic song "Rule Britannia" summed up the mood of the time.

1650 Corn is eaten for the first time in Italy as polenta, mashed corn meal, or hardened into a cake.

1666 Antonio Stradivari, Italian violin-maker, is established at Cremona; he will make instruments of unrivaled beauty and tone.

1700–1800 Indian Moslems introduce dyeing techniques to Indonesia, making multicolored batik fabrics possible.

1650~1750

Sonatas and Concertos
Italian Instrumental Music

By now you'll have gathered that opera and the Italian monodic style had quite an impact on music across seventeenth-century Europe. But the other elements of the Baroque style—contrast, harmony, bold melodic lines, ornamentation—were quietly being developed by a growing number of composers into new instrumental forms to suit orchestral forces and emergent chamber groups. By the end of the century there were several composers of concerti grossi, trio sonatas, and solo sonatas.

Concerto grosso—the new orchestral form.

WORKS **TO WATCH**

Corelli wrote comparatively little and all of it can be recommended, but a good introduction to his music is the "Christmas" concerto, which gets performed regularly. On the other hand, Vivaldi wrote loads, the best known being the violin concertos op.8 nos.1–4 (better known as *The Four Seasons*). It's all pretty good; don't miss his *Gloria* in D.

WORKS **TO WATCH**

So let's leave opera and even ignore the vast number of oratorios, cantatas, and madrigals by *Alessandro SCARLATTI* (1660–1725), and concentrate on instrumental music —because that's what the late Baroque in Italy is really all about.

Confusingly, the two pioneers of the new instrumental music were *Arcangelo CORELLI* (1653–1713) and *Giuseppe TORELLI* (1658–1709). Although they didn't invent the forms, it was their refinement of the concerto grosso and the trio sonata in particular that paved the way for the orchestral and chamber music of the next hundred years or so.

Stradivari's workshop in Cremona. His instruments are still being played today.

1711 The construction of the Zwinger Palace in Dresden begins, a triumph of Rococo style.

1715 The rate of literacy in Protestant northern Europe is 50 percent; in the Catholic south it is 25 percent or less.

1748 London physician John Fothergill's "Account of the Sore Throat Attended with Ulcers" is the first description of diphtheria.

A MAN FOR ALL SEASONS

But it was *Antonio VIVALDI* (1678–1741)—whose *Four Seasons* is played constantly across the world—who stole the show, writing brilliant concertos, over 500 of them, and numerous sonatas of all types. But hang on, what exactly are concertos? Well, the form derives from the Gabrielis' antiphonal style (Vivaldi was a Venetian too), contrasting two groups of instruments in a sort of dialogue. By Vivaldi's time, the concerto usually consisted of a string orchestra (plus continuo) and a smaller group of instruments (the *concertino*)—this combination was known as the concerto grosso; sometimes the concertino was reduced to a single solo instrument, creating a solo concerto.

NAMES TO NOTE

The generation after Corelli included a huge number of composers of concertos and sonatas. Vivaldi is the best known and most prolific, but there were plenty of others worth listening to—among them **Francesco Geminiani** *(1687–1762),* **Francesco Veracini** *(1690–1768),* **Giuseppe Tartini** *(1692–1770),* **Pietro Antonio Locatelli** *(1695–1764), and* **Giovanni Pergolesi** *(1710–36).* **Tomaso Giovanni Albinoni** *(1671–1751) wrote some fine instrumental music too, but beware— the famous* Adagio *is a twentieth-century fake.*

Viols to Violins

With any change in musical style there is usually a change in instrumentation too. The viols used in Renaissance consorts were not as well suited to the rhythmic Baroque style, and were being replaced by the newer violin family—among which were some fantastic instruments being made at the time by families such as the Amatis, Guarneris, and (greatest of all) Antonio Stradivari (1644–1737).

And the sonata? More complicated . . . it came in two forms: the *sonata da chiesa* (church sonata)—rather serious—and the *sonata da camera* (chamber sonata), usually a set of dances. A convention evolved of sonatas for two solo instruments plus continuo of bass instrument and keyboard, called a trio sonata (although it requires four players). Pieces for solo instruments were also called sonatas. One-movement keyboard sonatas constitute most of the work of *Domenico SCARLATTI* (1685–1757), and it's possible that his striking harmonies were intended for the new invention, the piano, rather than the harpsichord.

1683 Ottoman troops under the grand vizier Kara Mustapha lay siege to Vienna; the Turks are all but annihilated.

1686 Theatrical manager Johannes Velten produces a German version of *Hamlet, Der Bestrafte Brüdersmord*; his company will survive until 1771.

1709 Germans Johann Friedrich Böttger and Ehrenfried Walther von Tschirnhausen discover how to reproduce Chinese porcelain.

1680~1770

Eins, Zwei, Drei . . .

Late Baroque in Germany

George Frideric Handel, minus wig, composing at the keyboard.

German music in the seventeenth century, although magnificent, wasn't exactly fun. The influence of the Lutheran church was felt in all walks of life, the Thirty Years' War (1618–48) was taking its toll, and the music of the time reflected the somber atmosphere. Most of it, even the instrumental music, was religious in one way or another, in sharp contrast with the rise of secular forms written purely for entertainment elsewhere in Europe. By around 1700 it was time for a change, and three composers appeared who personified the various directions German music was to take.

A Reluctant Musician

Telemann first started composing in his teens, but being a sensible lad, decided to give it all up to study law at Leipzig University. Unfortunately, someone at the university came across a piece he'd written and persuaded him to write a bit more. He was soon commissioned to write a cantata every two weeks for St. Thomas's, the main church in Leipzig. Before he knew what was happening, he was appointed to various musical posts in the city, and Germany had lost a promising lawyer.

The greatest of these was undoubtedly *Johann Sebastian BACH* (1685–1750), an essentially conservative and intensely religious composer who continued in the tradition of Schütz and Buxtehude; on the other hand,

surpassing Bach in popularity at the time was *George Frideric HANDEL* (1685–1759), a cosmopolitan extrovert who felt quite at home with the new Italian styles. But let's leave these two giants for the time being and have a look at the third of the trio, who took a different path and in some ways was more forward-looking than his contemporaries.

George Frideric Handel.

1709 In Padua, Bartolomeo Cristofori constructs the first mechanism for a true pianoforte.

1718 New Orleans is founded by the French; the city's French influence will remain, especially in the Vieux Carré and in the celebration of Mardi Gras.

1770 Captain James Cook takes possession of New Holland (Australia) in the name of George III; the great variety of plants there leads Cook to name his landfall Botany Bay.

Georg Philipp TELEMANN (1681–1767) was not only the most popular composer in Germany in his own lifetime, but also wrote more than just about any other composer, before or since. Not all of it has survived, and some is not the greatest music ever written, but the vast majority shows a prodigious musical talent, so it's unfortunate that he has sometimes been neglected in favor of Bach and Handel.

Telemann was something of an eclectic. He wrote religious music in the German tradition, as well as French- and Italian-style instrumental music, but brought his own distinctive style to whatever he did. This was marked by an elegant simplicity and a tendency toward graceful melodies with understated accompaniment—avoiding both Germanic heaviness and Italianate ornamentation. In this respect he was a forerunner of the late eighteenth-century "classical" style, which we'll come

“ ☆ ”

Prolific Composers

For some reason, composers in the eighteenth century were particularly industrious. Joseph Haydn is famous for having written 104 symphonies, more than 80 string quartets, and hundreds of other chamber works, but he

So many, many notes.

pales into insignificance when compared with the output of Vivaldi (at least 21 operas, 500 concertos, about 90 sonatas), Luigi Boccherini (26 symphonies, 14 concertos, 48 string trios, 91 string quartets, 125 string quintets, and hundreds of other chamber pieces), J. S. Bach (well over 1,000 works of various kinds), and Telemann (about 45 operas, and huge quantities of instrumental and religious music).

across a bit later. The three collections of *Musique de table*, published in 1733, are his best-known works and include orchestral concertos, suites, and various chamber pieces, apparently designed as an accompaniment to dining out—rather superior Muzak.

Both Bach and Telemann were drawn to the musical center of Leipzig, Bach serving as *Kantor* at the Thomaskirche from 1723 until his death in 1750.

LIPSIAE INSIGNIS SAX oniæ urbis et celeberrimi Emporij vera Effigies. Ann. M.DC.XVII.

1685 Charles II dies, saying, "Let not poor Nelly starve," a reference to Nell Gwynn, an actress who was the king's mistress and mother of two of his illegitimate sons.

1705 Johann Sebastian Bach journeys 250 miles on foot to Lübeck to hear *Abendmusik* directed by the Danish-born organist and composer Dietrich Buxtehude.

1718 Leopold of Dessau invents the iron ramrod, which will be used to force the charge into a muzzle-loading firearm.

1685~1750

A Musical Upbringing
Johann Sebastian Bach: The Life

When musicians discuss J. S. Bach, the superlatives come thick and fast. Although he was considered to be rather conservative and dryly academic in his own time, he was rediscovered in the "Bach revival" of the nineteenth century, and became an icon to subsequent generations of composers. Quite simply, he was one of the greatest musical geniuses of all time.

J. S. B. at the harpsichord   *A little parental guidance*   *One of many Bach juniors*

J. S. Bach enjoyed family life, especially domestic music-making, which must have been second nature to this most musical of families.

TO WATCH

J. S. B.'s choral music is invariably first-rate, but there are works that are sublime: the *St. John* and *St. Matthew Passions*, the *Mass in B minor*, and the *Magnificat* are all unmissable. The *Christmas Oratorio*, and cantatas or motets such as *Wachet auf*, *Jesu meine Freude*, and the secular *Coffee Cantata* get regular performances.

WORKS

Johann Sebastian came from a very musical family and was destined to become a professional musician. When he left school, he took on a number of unsatisfactory jobs as "lackey-musician" and organist, and didn't really settle down until he became organist and chamber musician to the duke of Saxe-Weimar in 1708. During his nine years at Weimar, he wrote much of his best organ music and some cantatas but was denied promotion, and so applied for the post of *Kapellmeister* (musical director) at the court of Prince Leopold of Cöthen.

1728 Danish explorer Vitus Bering discovers the Bering Strait between Asia and North America.

1740 The city of Berlin has a population of nearly 70,000; in 1690 it was approximately 20,000.

1750 Massachusetts has 63 distilleries making rum from molasses. Slave traders sell them the molasses and use the money to buy more African slaves, whom they sell to West Indian sugar planters.

THE BACH FAMILY

The Bach family tree has been traced back as far as the sixteenth century, and of the eighty or so male members up to 1850, only a handful were not musicians. Most were called Johann something, so it can be confusing, but the ones to watch out for are: Johann Sebastian, and his sons Wilhelm Friedemann (1710–84), Carl Philipp Emanuel (1714–88), Johann Christoph Friederich (1732–95), and Johann Christian (1735–82).

His departure from Weimar was acrimonious—the duke refused to accept his resignation and imprisoned him for a month before sacking him—but his new employer made the move worthwhile. The court was Calvinist, so music played little part in worship, but Bach got on well with Leopold, who was a talented musician. At Cöthen, Bach concentrated mainly on instrumental music for the court, and also keyboard pieces—including many written as exercises for his growing family.

After his first wife, Maria Barbara, died, Bach married the singer Anna Magdalena Wilcke. The prince also took the plunge—but the new princess's lack of interest in music led J. S. B. to look for yet another job, this time as *Kantor* at the prestigious St. Thomas's School in Leipzig, a post which he held from 1723 until his death. His duties at Leipzig included providing music for the city's two main churches, and it was here that he wrote most of his finest choral work, as well as various collections of chamber and keyboard music.

> ### " ☆ "
> ### *BWV, K, RV, Op., etc.*
> You may notice the letters BWV, plus a number, after the title of many of Bach's pieces. This refers to the *Bach-Werke-Verzeichnis*, a catalogue compiled by Wolfgang Schmieder that helps to sort out which work is which. Similar catalogues exist for the works of Vivaldi (which have RV numbers) and Mozart (K, or Köchel, numbers), but most other composers' output is catalogued chronologically by opus (or op.) numbers.

Throughout his varied musical career, Bach composed in almost every genre except opera, providing music for the demands of his employers. But his intense religious convictions suffuse even his instrumental pieces—he dedicated all his work "To the Greater Glory of God."

J. S. Bach, composer, performer, and organ consultant, snatches a moment to pose for a portrait . . .

1686 At Mme. de Maintenon's Institut de Saint-Louis, a school for the daughters of impoverished nobles, cookery is taught and the Cordon Bleu is awarded to graduates.

1700–1800 The synthetic pigment "Prussian blue" is discovered in Germany; by 1900, the number of pigments available to artists will be doubled.

1714 On the death of Queen Anne, the last monarch of the House of Stuart, Prince George Louis of Hanover, who speaks no English, becomes George I of England.

1685~1750

The Well-Tempered Musician
Johann Sebastian Bach

Quite apart from the sheer volume Bach produced, a couple of things put him head and shoulders above most other composers: superb craftsmanship, resulting from rigorous study and a staggering intellect; and a profoundly spiritual sensitivity. But he was no ivory-tower figure, and somehow found the time to enjoy life to the full, especially as the proud father of 20 children. His music is satisfying on all levels, academic and emotional, and it is perhaps the balance between heart and head that gives it its enduring universality.

It is as well to remember that Bach considered his talent to be a gift from God, and that throughout his life he remained a staunch Lutheran. Church music was an important part of his *oeuvre*, and Lutheran chorales figure large in much of his music—as themes for chorale preludes for the organ written in Weimar, as well as in his sacred choral music. He harmonized hundreds of chorale tunes for congregational singing. In Leipzig he had

B, A, C, H

The German system of letter-names for notes is somewhat different from the English, and includes (conveniently) the letter H. This meant that Johann Sebastian could "sign" his name using the four notes B, A, C, H (the English B flat, A, C, B natural)—a motif found in several of his works, especially the *Art of Fugue*. Not many composers could do that, but Bach explored the musical version of his name with typical thoroughness.

Bach's music was "rediscovered" in the nineteenth century, especially through Mendelssohn's influential advocacy.

1740 Publication of Samuel Richardson's epistolary novel *Pamela, or Virtue Rewarded*, extolling a virtuous maidservant's resistance to her lecherous master's advances.

1747 French mathematician Jean Le Rond d'Alembert researches vibrating strings.

1752 Britain adopts the Gregorian calendar (introduced in Europe in 1582); the loss of 11 days causes confusion and riots when people claim wages for the lost days.

to write a cantata for each Sunday service (over 200 have survived), but also managed to produce two full-length settings of the *Passion* for choir, soloists, and orchestra, as well as the *Mass in B minor* and numerous other one-off pieces. Although these were written to order, Bach's dedication and sincerity never wavered, and they represent the pinnacle of Baroque church music.

The other side of Bach is best seen in the music he wrote in Cöthen, when he didn't have the opportunity to compose for the church. This period produced some brilliant orchestral music in the Italian style, including concertos and suites, and all sorts of music for the harpsichord or clavichord, including suites in the French and Italian styles, and the first volume of the *Well-Tempered Clavier*. This was a collection of 24 preludes and fugues—one of each in all the major and minor keys— which with the second book (finished in 1742) are known simply as "the 48." These, and his other keyboard pieces, show Bach's mastery of the techniques of counterpoint, but the collections of instrumental music written in his final years at Leipzig—the *Goldberg Variations*, the *Musical Offering*, and the *Art of Fugue*—combine technical brilliance with spiritual profundity in a summation of his lifelong devotion to God and music.

"☆"

A Royal Theme

Bach was famous for his ability to improvise at the keyboard. When he visited Frederick the Great in 1747, the king wrote a theme for him to play around with. Bach liked it so much he used it as the basis of the collection of fugues, canons, and sonatas he called the *Musical Offering*.

The manuscript of the *Art of Fugue*, unfinished at Bach's death, with an explanatory comment by his son C. P. E. Bach.

Cellist battling with one of the solo *Suites*.

1711 English trumpeter and lutenist John Shore invents the tuning fork.

1717 Lady Mary Wortley Montagu, English letter-writer and wit, describes "engrafting" in Adrianople, an early form of inoculation against smallpox.

1726 Jonathan Swift predicts in *Gulliver's Travels* not only that Mars has two moons, but the times of their respective revolutions; this will be confirmed in 1877.

1685~1759

The Harmonious Tunesmith
Handel's Instrumental Music

Born just four weeks before J. S. Bach, in a nearby part of Lutheran Germany, George Frideric Handel also showed early signs of musical talent. But there the similarities end. While Bach was brought up in a musical family and remained in Germany composing music mainly in the German tradition, Handel had to study music in secret (his father wanted him to be a lawyer) and traveled widely, assimilating the latest styles from all over Europe, eventually settling in London. And while Bach actively avoided opera, Handel made his name in the field of dramatic music. The one thing they shared was a phenomenal musical ability.

WORKS

TO WATCH

For sheer exuberance, the *Water Music* and *Music for the Royal Fireworks* are hard to beat, but the 12 concerti grossi op. 6 give a better idea of Handel's breadth of style, and the organ concertos op. 4 are worth a try too. Of the keyboard music, the most popular is the E major suite, which includes the air and variations later saddled with the nickname "*The Harmonious Blacksmith.*"

TO WATCH

WORKS

Handel started out as a church organist in his home town of Halle, but soon gave this up for the bright lights of Hamburg, where he played violin and harpsichord at the opera house. He was still a young man when his first operas were performed there in 1705, and their success brought him an invitation to tour Italy for the next three years, mastering the Italian style of opera and oratorio and getting a reputation as a musical whiz kid. When he returned to Germany he was appointed *Kapellmeister* to the elector of Hanover, but he'd

Handel's birthplace in Halle, with one of his elegant two-manual harpsichords.

1750 In London John Fielding and his novelist brother Henry found the Bow Street Runners, precursors of the police force.

1756 Robert Clive's victory over the nawab of Bengal at Plassey definitively establishes British power in India.

1760 New Jonathan in London's Threadneedle Stre displays the sign "Stock Exchange"; it is one of several coffee shops where dealers transact business.

George I knew how to throw a party, and commissioned Handel to write a suitable accompaniment for the pyrotechnics.

acquired a taste for travel and took several leaves of absence to stage his operas in London. He never returned from his final trip, in 1712—but he was presumably forgiven for going AWOL, as the elector later became George I of England, and granted Handel a fat pension.

Handel didn't only write operas and oratorios. He was a talented keyboard player and composed a fair amount for organ and harpsichord, but had also picked up on the fashion for orchestral music in France and Italy. Perhaps his most famous works are the orchestral suite *Water Music*, written for a party George I held on the Thames River, and the *Music for the Royal Fireworks* to celebrate the Peace of Aix-la-Chapelle, both good examples of Handel the showman. He also wrote several sets of impressive concerti grossi and concertos for organ, which show a gift for tunefulness and originality, as do his sonatas for flute, recorder, and violin with continuo.

Public Concerts

One thing that helped Handel to achieve superstar status was the rise of opera houses and concert halls, built specially for that purpose, in the eighteenth century. In previous eras classical music had been restricted to the courts and churches, or amateur performances staged at home. Amazingly, concerts open to the public only appeared in the eighteenth century, but fast became a popular middle-class entertainment.

1685 French Huguenots begin emigrating following the restoration of the Edict of Nantes.

1695 The University of Berlin is established.

1700 Captain William Kidd is captured and arrested on charges of piracy. He is hanged the following year.

1685~1759

Hallelujah!
Handel's Choral Music

Purcell's untimely death in 1695 left a huge gap in British music, just when a distinctive English operatic style was beginning to evolve. The public had developed quite an appetite for opera and oratorio, but no English composer was up to taking over where Purcell left off; so when Handel arrived in London he was welcomed with open arms. Okay, he wasn't English, and he wrote Italian-style operas, but what the heck—this guy was good.

Handel, the German who became England's greatest composer of Italian music.

And he knew when he was on to a good thing, too. He had had enthusiastic audiences for his operas in Italy, but England offered him the chance to really make it big. His opera *Rinaldo* was a huge hit in London in 1711, and he followed it with several more, hoping for the same sort of success. But although the public loved his music, they were not always happy about opera sung in Italian, and the operas got a mixed reception.

" ☆ "

Such Stuff As Dreams Are Made Of

Such is the popularity of *Messiah* that nearly every local choir or choral society performs it on a regular basis, and many musicians think they could play it in their sleep. One cellist, so the story goes, even dreamt that he was playing *Messiah* yet again, and woke up to find that he was …

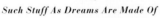

The Royal Academy of Music—not to be confused with the later teaching establishment—was founded in 1720 to promote Italian opera, with Handel

1732 London's Theatre Royal in Covent Garden opens with the Congreve comedy *The Way of the World*.

1759 German scientist Kaspar Friedrich Wolff observes the development of growing plants.

as its musical director. He wrote a series of operas for it, but eventually it was a financial failure and folded in 1728. He continued to compose operas until 1741, including some of his finest pieces, such as *Orlando*, but became increasingly disillusioned and financially insecure.

So, although his main interest was always opera, Handel concentrated more on the typical English forms of ode, anthem, and particularly oratorio. *Messiah*

The original score of Handel's *Messiah*, a perennial favorite.

TO WATCH

WORKS

Handel's operas didn't get the success they deserved in his lifetime, but they're much more appreciated these days. Look out for performances of *Giulio Cesare*, *Serse* (Xerxes), and *Orlando*, which are enjoying a revival. As for the oratorios, you're really spoiled for choice: *Messiah*, with its famous Hallelujah chorus, is a must, but just as appealing are *Judas Maccabeus*, *Saul*, and *Israel in Egypt*. And for really uplifting stuff, try the anthems written for the coronation of George III, which include the popular *Zadok the Priest*.

TO WATCH

A performance of *Messiah* in Handel's favorite venue —the Foundling Hospital for Charity. The great tradition of *Messiah* performances started here.

was a turning point in his career, a masterpiece that contains elements of all his mature style, and the high point of Baroque oratorio composition—and one of the most frequently performed choral works even now. When it was premiered in Dublin in 1742 to rave reviews, Handel gave up on opera completely and devoted the rest of his life to English oratorio, a form he made his own. He wrote and performed in 12 more oratorios, mainly to Old Testament texts (such as *Samson* and *Solomon*), but also some based on classical mythology (*Semele* and *Hercules*), often playing his own organ concertos in the interval. Failing health and blindness cut short his musical activity in the 1750s, but when he died in 1759 he was acknowledged as the greatest composer of his time, and was buried in Westminster Abbey.

emorable lines
· singers ...

, and
strumentalists

The ubiquitous basso continuo

Digression

Seated One Day at the Keyboard ...

The popularity of instruments such as the organ and harpsichord in the Renaissance and Baroque periods can be explained by the

fact that they can play several notes at a time, and so made ideal solo instruments. In fact, it also made them perfect for accompaniment. The unifying feature of all keyboard instruments is, it almost goes without saying, the keyboard of black and white notes, pressed to activate some kind of sound-producing mechanism. But that's sometimes the only thing members of the keyboard family have in common.

A decorated pipe organ
built in about 1600.

THE ORGAN

The oldest member of the family, dating back to ancient Greece, is the organ, which the British conductor Sir Thomas Beecham described as "a mechanical box of whistles." Air is pumped into the organ by bellows (or nowadays an electrical pump) and allowed to pass through pipes or reeds when the keys are pressed. Organs range in size from the medieval portative organ, which was pumped with the left hand and played with the right, to massive beasts with several ranks of pipes and reeds, a set of pedal-operated keys at the organist's feet, and two or three rows of keyboards.

THE HARPSICHORD

The first harpsichords appeared in the fifteenth century, and reached the height of their popularity in the Baroque period. Basically, the harpsichord is a resonating box containing stretched wire

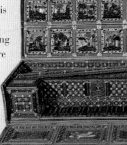

Virginals were popular for amateur music-making in the Elizabethan period.

Menu of available sounds

Familiar piano-style keyboard

Modern electronic keyboards offer a whole range of sounds.

strings that are plucked by quills, via a mechanism operated by the keyboard. The smaller virginal and spinet, which were designed as domestic instruments, operate on the same principle and have a similar sound. The one drawback of these plucked-string keyboard instruments is that no matter how hard or softly the keys are struck, the volume of the note is the same, making expressive performance difficult. This is why they were eventually superseded by the more flexible piano.

THE PIANO

Another popular Baroque instrument was the clavichord; unlike the harpsichord, its strings are struck (not plucked) by metal "tangents" on the end of the keys, allowing some control over the volume produced. Unfortunately, the clavichord was only capable of soft, very soft, and virtually inaudible, so when *Bartolomeo* CRISTOFORI (1655–1731) took the insides out of harpsichords and replaced them with an action that struck the strings with leather-covered wooden hammers, he had really found a gap in the market. The *gravicembalo*

col piano e forte (harpsichord with soft and loud) he invented in about 1700 was the first grand piano, and the modern version differs only in details, for example, the hammers are now felt-covered, and the body is reinforced with an iron frame. Early pianos are, for some peculiar reason, often known as fortepianos, and various shapes, including the so-called square piano, were tried until makers settled on the familiar grand and the domestic upright.

ELECTRONICS

The twentieth century brought electronic wizardry into musical instrument technology, but it made sense for the new instruments to be operated from the now-familiar keyboard. Two inventions of the 1920s, the Theremin (which doesn't have a keyboard—it's played by mysteriously waving your hands around near the instrument) and the Ondes Martenot, were the precursors of the modern electronic organ and the synthesizer, both of which produce electronically generated sounds at the touch of the keys.

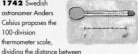

1731 The earliest known public concert in North America takes place in Boston, Massachusetts.

1742 Swedish astronomer Anders Celsius proposes the 100-division thermometer scale, dividing the distance between freezing (0°C) and boiling (100°C).

1755 Giovanni Casanova returns to Venice and is imprisoned as a spy; he has spent 14 years traveling through Europe as a preacher, alchemist, gambler, and musician.

1740~1800

Enlightenment
From Baroque to Classical

Christoph Gluck.

The music of Bach and Handel marked the climax of the Baroque, and the end of an era. The eighteenth century was the period of the Enlightenment, rationalism, and humanitarianism, and the arts reflected this. Public concerts were attracting a new audience, who wanted an entertaining style of music with more clearly defined structures. The dense textures and intense counterpoint of the Baroque were being replaced by the French Rococo and gallant styles, characterized by gracefulness of line and elegance of structure, which had their roots in the works of Couperin, Rameau, and Domenico Scarlatti. By 1750 a new style was emerging, which, because of its emphasis on form and balance, became known as "classical."

Frederick the Great

We have a couple of enthusiastic (and wealthy) amateurs to thank for much of the music of this era—the elector of the Palatinate at Mannheim, and Frederick the Great. Frederick's patronage helped not only young C. P. E .Bach and his half-brother W. F., but also many other leading musicians of the time.

Although the new style originated in France and Italy, the musical center of Europe was shifting to Germany and Austria, and eventually settled in Vienna. One of the first composers to break with the Baroque tradition was *Christoph Willibald GLUCK* (1714–87), a German who felt uncomfortable with the artifice of Italian-style opera. He wanted to achieve a more realistic portrayal of human emotions, rather than mythological cavortings, and developed a

1760 The famous Irish-born beauty Lady Coventry dies, a victim of cosmetics; she has used "ceruse," a preparation containing corrosive white lead.

1773 Sturm und Drang; Johann Wolfgang Goethe's Götz von Berlichingen is the first German play inspired by Shakespeare.

1804 German promoter Frederick Albert Winsor demonstrates gas lighting at London's Lyceum Theatre.

style of "reform opera." His aim, clarity of expression, was typical of Enlightenment thinking, and the essence of classical style.

Exciting things were happening in the field of orchestral music too. An orchestra was established in Mannheim by the new elector, who had the money to indulge his passion for music. He employed the best musicians available and several composers (an assemblage that became known as the Mannheim School) to work with the orchestra; among them was the young *Johann STAMITZ* (1717–57). Stamitz wrote more than 50 symphonies during his career, developing a style of orchestral writing that was in marked contrast to the concerto grosso developed by the previous generation of composers.

NAMES TO NOTE

Early classical music sometimes gets overlooked, being sandwiched between Bach/Handel and Haydn/Mozart, but keep your ears open for **Giovanni Battista Martini** *(1706–84), who taught J. C. Bach and the young Mozart;* **Giovanni Battista Sammartini** *(c.1700–1775);* **Johann Georg Albrechtsberger** *(1736–89), who taught Beethoven; and* **Carl Ditters von Dittersdorf** *(1739–99), who wrote more than 120 symphonies.*

The Crescendo

Just as the Gabrielis had made a feature of the contrast between loud and soft passages, Stamitz and the Mannheim composers were famous for the introduction of long orchestral crescendos, gradual increases in volume, to reach a thrilling climax. Another exciting effect that became something of a trademark was a rapid upward phrase, which became known as the "Mannheim rocket."

Frederick the Great was a gifted flautist, and often joined in with the court orchestra.

If J. S. Bach's time was now up, his sons continued the family musical tradition—taking it toward the new classical style. Four of them became musicians of talent: *Wilhelm Friedemann* (1710–84) and *Johann Christoph Friederich* (1732–95) had modest success as composers; *Carl Philipp Emanuel* (1714–88), best known for his keyboard sonatas and fantasias, and *Johann Christian* (1735–82), who wrote operas, and orchestral and chamber music, were both considered among the finest composers of their day.

1740 Charles VI, the last Hapsburg emperor, dies; over the next eight years, the War of the Austrian Succession will involve most of Europe's great powers.

1761 The ballet *Don Juan*, with music by the composer Christoph Gluck, is presented in Vienna by Gasparo Angiolini, ballet master to the Austrian Imperial Theaters.

1767 Mozart's first dramatic work, *Die Schuldigkeit des Ersten Gebotes*, is performed in Austria; the composer is 11.

1750~c.1825

Classical Classical Music
Austria

Vienna

It was no accident that Austria should become such a center for musical activity in the late eighteenth century. It is geographically right in the middle of Europe, ideally placed to be a melting pot for the various styles appearing in Italy, north Germany, France, and Bohemia. And besides, the bourgeoisie there had loads of money to throw around on their many and varied cultural hobbies.

The "Age of Enlightenment" harked back to the ideals of ancient Greece and Rome, and the discovery of the ruins of Pompeii in 1748 revived interest in all things classical. Architects were returning to clean lines, and composers were attempting to re-create the music of Orpheus and Pythagoras (though they hadn't a clue what it actually sounded like) by emphasizing formal elements and omitting what they saw as the vulgar ornamentation and indulgent expressiveness that typified the Baroque.

The discovery of the ruins of Pompeii stimulated a revival of interest in all things classical.

The contrapuntal intricacies of the old style were seen as an extravagance and were replaced by straightforward melody and accompaniment; and the expressive harmonies and dramatic contrasts of the Baroque were supplanted by simple chords and homogeneity. Composers of the classical period were not so much interested in personal expression as in clarity and, above all, elegance.

1785 French botanist Antoine Parmentier presents a bouquet of potato flowers to Louis XVI to encourage their cultivation.

1791 French novelist and pornographer the Marquis de Sade writes *Justine ou les malheurs de la vertu.*

1820s Typhoid fever, an acute infectious disease caused by the bacillus *Salmonella typhi* and transmitted by contaminated milk, water, or food, is distinguished from typhus.

THE C WORD

The use of the term "classical music" to describe art music in general probably came about when the concert repertoire consisted largely of music from the classical period (Haydn/Mozart/ Beethoven)—which to some extent it still does.

Even when used specifically for that period it's something of a misnomer, because really the term refers to ancient Greece and Rome. But we're stuck with it now, more's the pity.

Compared with previous movements in music, the classical era was short-lived, lasting from around 1750 to the 1820s, but many of the innovations of the period had a profound influence on later styles. The forms that evolved became the basis for much of the music for the next hundred years and more. The orchestra expanded to include a full complement of woodwind instruments (including the newly invented clarinet) and even some brass and percussion, and the piano took over from the harpsichord. Gone was the ubiquitous continuo, which was too fussy to have any place in the new elegant style.

Most important, though, were the composers who were attracted to Vienna, which had become the musical capital of the Western world. Musicians were no longer trooping off to Italy to study. In fact, the situation was quite the reverse.

The restraint and coolness of the classical style particularly suited the Germanic temperament, and composers from Germany and Austria-Hungary began to dominate the musical scene.

NAMES TO NOTE

You'd be forgiven for thinking that Haydn, Mozart, and Beethoven were the only composers around at this time, but there's some lovely stuff by **Domenico Cimarosa (1749–1801)**, **Muzio Clementi (1752–1832)**, *and* **Luigi Cherubini (1760–1842)** *that has been unfairly neglected. And keep an ear open for* **John Field (1782–1837)**, *an Irish pianist credited with the invention of the nocturne.*

Among them were three men who stood out as the greatest composers of their—and arguably all—time: *Joseph HAYDN (1732–1809)*, *Wolfgang Amadeus MOZART (1756–91)*, and *Ludwig van BEETHOVEN (1770–1827)*. This trio dominated the scene, and their music still forms the backbone of the classical repertoire.

The four-year-old Mozart delights the crowds at the wedding of Joseph II and Isabella of Parma, 1760.

1749–56 Swedish philosopher, scientist, and mystic Emanuel Swedenborg publishes *Arcana Coelestia*, propounding an allegorical interpretation of the Scriptures.

1770 English weaver-mechanic James Hargreaves patents the spinning jenny, beginning the process of automation in the textile industry.

1774 Goethe's *Sorrows of Young Werther* recounts the sufferings and suicide of a sensitive artist; Werther's blue coat, yellow breeches, and romantic melancholy are widely imitated.

1732~1809

Tea and Symphony
Haydn and Patronage

Haydn's parents were only amateurs, but encouraged their son's early interest in music.

Joseph Haydn was born in 1732, when J. S. Bach and Handel were at the height of their careers, and died in 1809, the year Beethoven wrote his fifth piano concerto. The 50 or so years of his active composing life form a bridge between the Baroque and the beginnings of Romanticism, two staggeringly different musical worlds. Despite his somewhat conventional career as a court composer, Haydn was a great innovator, expanding and perfecting the forms of the symphony and string quartet, and his later works show the sort of emotional expression that became a hallmark of nineteenth-century music.

TO WATCH

WORKS

All Haydn's music is well crafted, but a lot of the early stuff is really only for entertainment—a sort of eighteenth-century Muzak. He came into his own by about 1770, and symphonies 26, 39, and 44 are really serious and original works. The six string quartets op. 20, and six op. 33, also show the development of a highly individual style.

WORKS

TO WATCH

Although he didn't come from a particularly musical family, Haydn became a chorister at St. Stephen's Cathedral in Vienna at the age of eight. He virtually taught himself composition by studying the works of C. P. E. Bach, and worked as a violinist and teacher until he got his first post as *Kapellmeister* with Count Maximilian von Morzin. But the big break came in 1761 when he was appointed second *Kapellmeister* to the Esterházy family, becoming full *Kapellmeister* to Prince Nikolaus in 1766.

“ ☆ ”

Marry in Haste, Repent at Leisure

Haydn may have been well loved as a musician, but his marriage was a disaster. He fell in love with one of his pupils in Vienna, but when she became a nun, he foolishly married her sister—who had no ear for music and was an utterly unsuitable partner. They separated, childless, and Haydn spent the rest of his life sending her money.

1789 Erasmus Darwin's long poem "The Loves of the Plants" embodies the botanic system of Linnaeus.

1793 Lazare Carnot introduces the *levée en masse*; universal military conscription in France is seen as both a Republican duty and a necessity for national survival.

1808 German romantic painter Caspar David Friedrich makes his first oil paintings; his land- and seascapes suggest melancholy, isolation, and human powerlessness.

ESTERHÁZA

Having a regular income, an enthusiastic employer, and talented musicians at his disposal, Haydn settled down to write an enormous amount of music. At the magnificent Esterházy estate in Eisenstadt, he directed about 20 musicians (who loved working with him and gave him the nickname "Papa Haydn"), producing symphonies and quartets for the twice-weekly concerts and the prince's *Tafelmusik* (music to eat by) and a large number of trios featuring the baryton (a kind of viol), which was the prince's instrument. An opera house was opened at Esterháza in

Haydn's Musical Jokes

The respectability of the classical style can get wearisome, so it's just as well that Haydn didn't always take things too seriously. For example, the "Surprise" symphony (no.94) was intended to wake up the dozing audience, and the "Farewell" symphony (no.45), in which the players leave the stage one by one, was a hint that the orchestra could do with a vacation.

Joseph Haydn.

1768, and Haydn wrote several operas for the place, but his reputation was mainly founded on instrumental music.

Much of his early music was in the same mold as that of the Mannheim composers and C. P. E. Bach, and Haydn could easily have rested on his laurels and continued writing in the conventional classical style. But the resources available to him at Esterháza inspired him to go a bit further, and to translate some of the revolutionary thinking of the period into musical terms; Haydn's lifetime saw the declaration of republics in France and the U.S., and his middle symphonies are roughly contemporary with the Boston Tea Party.

The grand Esterházy palace at Eisenstadt, where Haydn was given free rein to develop his own style of composition.

1729 Johann Sebastian Bach's *St. Matthew Passion* is first performed in Germany.

1759 French controller-general Etienne de Silhouette unsuccessfully attempts financial reforms, giving birth to the derisive word "silhouette," meaning "a figure reduced to its simplest form."

1773 A cargo of English tea is dumped into Boston Harbor by American radicals, an event known as the Boston Tea Party.

1732 ~ 1809

Papa Haydn

Haydn's Mature Works

TO WATCH

WORKS

Just about all the late instrumental works are worth a hearing, but perhaps the best known are symphonies nos. 94 ("Surprise") and 10 ("London"), the six op. 76 string quarter and the brilliant trumpet concerto. B absolutely unmissab are the big choral works: the "Nelson" mass and the two great oratorios *The Creation* and *The Seasons.*

WORK

Haydn was tied to Esterháza for most of the time, only occasionally taking a short break in Vienna, so didn't often get the opportunity to hear what was going on in the rest of the musical world. Despite the lack of external influence on his music, he developed a style of his own, constantly experimenting and improving his technique. He also had the good fortune to have an orchestra to play these experiments, so that he could see what worked and what didn't. As he put it himself, "cut off from the world . . . I was forced to be original."

Trying out Haydn's latest chamber work at Esterháza.

By about 1770 he had outgrown the fashionable idea of music as light entertainment, and tried to achieve something with more depth. He was influenced in his thinking by the literary and artistic *Sturm und Drang* (storm and stress) movement, which advocated a subjective expression of emotions, and wrote a series of symphonies (nos. 32 to about 52) that are more serious in character, and often in minor keys. It's possible Prince Nikolaus found them a bit heavy going (Haydn lightened up somewhat after that), but they were enormously popular elsewhere. By the 1780s he had renegotiated his contract to allow publication of his music, and his reputation spread across Europe, prompting the commission of the six "Paris" symphonies, nos. 82–87.

At the same time, he was working on the string quartets op. 33, which established the genre in the repertoire and were said to be in "a quite new and special manner"— presumably because of their idiomatic writing for the instruments. He had met Mozart on a trip to Vienna in 1781, and the two got on famously: Mozart was so influenced by Haydn's quartet writing that he dedicated a set of his own quartets to him, and Haydn returned the compliment with his set of op. 50.

Prince Nikolaus died in 1790, releasing Haydn from musical duties to the family (although he still drew a salary!) other than writing masses annually for the princess's nameday. He traveled to London twice, at the request of the impresario J. P. Salomon, with considerable popular and financial success. He conducted a number of concerts and wrote many new works for performance in London, including the last 12 symphonies for performance there, and four sets of string quartets for concert performance. But his final years were spent on the two magnificent oratorios *The Creation* and *The Seasons*—inspired no doubt by Handel, but stretching the classical idiom to its expressive limits, and demonstrating Haydn's absolute mastery.

Headless Haydn

A short footnote (headnote?) that Haydn probably would have enjoyed. He was originally buried in Vienna, but was reinterred at Eisenstadt in 1820. Unfortunately, his head went missing during the move, and appeared later on exhibition in Vienna. It was finally reunited with the rest of his body in 1954.

NICKNAMED WORKS

Many of Haydn's symphonies and string quartets have acquired amusing and unusual nicknames. Some, such as the "Surprise" (no. 94), "Military" (100), and "Farewell" (45) symphonies, are descriptive. Others, such as the "London" symphony (104), refer to their first performances. Bizarrely, when a chandelier fell into the audience, injuring nobody, after the first performance of symphony no.102, the nickname "Miracle" was promptly given to symphony no.96. The "Nelson" mass was so called after the latter's decisive victory at the Battle of the Nile.

A performance of *The Creation* on Haydn's 76th birthday.

Digression

Forms and Genres

Before we go any further, it might help to look at how a piece of music is constructed. It enhances appreciation of the composer's art if you can see a work as a whole, rather than just enjoying each moment as it comes, and it helps to focus your listening if you can make out a coherent shape. You can often pick up listening tips, like how many movements a piece has, from concert programs and sleeve notes—if you can decipher them—but you need to know the jargon of musical form. We've already seen how notes can be put together to make melody, harmony, and counterpoint, but that's only half the story. Melodies and phrases can be used as building blocks, known as themes, to give an organized structure to a piece of music.

Musical forms range from the simple theme and variations (which is pretty self-explanatory), through binary form (two themes, stated one after the other, and perhaps repeated), and ternary form (theme A, followed by theme B, then theme A once more) to rondo form (ABACAD, etc.) and sonata form, which is one of the most sophisticated of all. In simple terms, sonata form consists of an *exposition* in which two contrasting themes are presented, a *development* in which the composer plays around with the two themes, and a *recapitulation* when the two themes are played once more. Any one of these forms can be

Illustration for a ballet to Debussy's *L'Après-midi d'un faune.*

used on its own, or as a movement in a larger genre such as the symphony.

ORCHESTRAL GENRES

The conventional orchestral concert often follows a standard pattern of overture (a one-movement piece, often in sonata form), concerto (usually a three-movement, fast-slow-fast piece for soloist and orchestra), and then symphony (classically a four-movement work, with a sonata-form first movement, a slow movement, a minuet in ternary form, and a finale), and, if you're lucky, a lighter dance piece or the like as an encore. Of course, not all concerts follow this format, and you may get a symphonic poem or a suite of ballet music thrown in, but those are the major genres you're likely to come across.

CHAMBER AND SOLO GENRES

Chamber music concerts and solo recitals are more of a mixed bag—you name it, you can hear it—and vary according to the ensemble or instrument. Most common are trio sonatas, with their characteristic fast-slow-fast movements, and string quartets, which are multimovement pieces rather like symphonies in miniature, although similar forms exist for all sorts of combinations of instruments. There are also sonatas for solo instruments with or without piano accompaniment, and solo piano sonatas, which tend to be in three movements—typically, a sonata form, a ternary form, and a rondo.

Illustrated cover of the vocal score of Puccini's opera *Gianni Schicchi*.

VOCAL GENRES

A lot of choral music derives from church forms such as the mass and requiem, and the single-movement motet or anthem, as we've seen. In cantatas, oratorios, and passions, the choral sections are often separated by sections of recitative and solo arias, which are usually in ternary form. Song recitals regularly include arias from religious works and opera, but are mainly made up of songs (or ayres, chansons, or lieder) with keyboard or similar accompaniment. You'll also come across the "song cycle," a collection of songs with a theme or story.

In Britain, church and cathedral choirs—traditionally using boy sopranos instead of women—preserve the traditions of liturgical music.

| 1754 The war between the French and the English in North America ends in 1763 with the French losing Canada and the American Midwest to Britain. | 1757 Musician and amateur astronomer William Herschel comes to England to follow a musical career; in 1781 he will discover the planet Uranus. | 1762 English dandy Beau Nash dies; he has made Bath a fashionable watering place, brought dueling into disrepute, and civilized men's fashions. |

1756~1791

Who's a Clever Boy, Then?

Young Mozart

Wolfgang Amadeus Mozart's life was a tragically short one, but he started his musical career early. Very early. His father, Leopold, was an aspiring composer who recognized the amazing potential (musical and financial) in his son, and gave up his own career to thrust the infant Wolfgang and his sister Maria Anna onto the concert circuit. The poor prodigies were paraded in front of the crowned heads of Europe when Wolfgang was only five and Maria Anna ("Nannerl") only eleven. During these tours of Munich, Paris, London, and Italy, Wolfgang assimilated many of the different styles of music he heard, and began composing himself.

Mozart senior basks in the reflected glory of Wolfgang and Nannerl in Paris.

Mozart's Prodigious Talents

Young Wolfgang showed phenomenal musical ability, which was thoroughly exploited by his father. He was a proficient harpsichordist by the age of four, and on his tours of Europe he was improvising on themes supplied by the audience. Soon he was proficient at the violin as well. He also had a fantastic musical memory, and is reputed to have written out the entire score of Allegri's *Miserere* after only one hearing in 1770.

As you might expect, although remarkable for a boy of his age, his early compositions were rather derivative. The first pieces considered to be part of the repertoire were written in about 1773, but he had already written composed symphonies and the occasional instrumental *divertimenti*, harpsichord pieces, four settings of the mass, a couple of *Singspiele* (light operas), and two full-scale operas by then. Not bad for a teenager.

By this time, Mozart (or at least his dad) was looking for a full-time post where he could further exploit his talents. His job-seeking in Vienna was unsuccessful, but instead he came across

Wolfgang Amadeus Mozart.

1766 Franz Joseph Haydn becomes full *Kapellmeister* to Prince Esterházy of Hungary and will hold the position until 1790.

1775 The piano begins to take over from the harpsichord as an accompanying instrument; it is a more flexible instrument and can be played softly (*piano*) or loudly (*forte*).

1784 German philosopher Immanuel Kant's *Was Ist Aufklärung* summarizes the ideas of the "Age of Reason."

Haydn's music, which inspired him to write in a similar style—leading to his two first great symphonies, nos. 25 in G minor, K183, and 29 in A, K201. He eventually found work in Salzburg as concertmaster in the prince-archbishop's court in 1775, where he wrote some music for the church, a few light orchestral pieces, and his first violin and piano concertos. But this was not good enough for Leopold, who wanted fame and fortune for his son, so Wolfgang was sent off to Munich, Mannheim, and Paris, composing all the way, but ending up back in Salzburg in 1779.

Working for the prince-archbishop, he was denied the opportunity of writing opera, which was in those days the way to make it big. His chance came with a commission in 1780, which resulted in his first operatic success, *Idomeneo*, performed in Munich in January 1781. Having discovered a taste for the high life, Mozart resigned from his post (or maybe was sacked—he wasn't the most cooperative of employees) and left for the bright lights of Vienna in 1781, with, as he put it, "a kick on my arse . . . by order of our prince-archbishop." Not exactly a glowing reference, but a hint of the way forward for Mozart.

WORKS TO WATCH

A lot of Mozart's early music is fairly lightweight: for example, the "Haffner" serenade K250, *Eine kleine Nachtmusik*, and some of the *Divertimenti*—beautifully crafted, but hardly profound. But he wrote some masterpieces in his teens and early twenties too: the serenades for wind instruments K361 and K388, both of which show depths untouched in most of the earlier serenades; symphony 25 in G minor K183; the piano concerto K271 and the violin concertos K2167, 218, and 219.

TO WATCH WORKS

"☆"

Shafts of Wit

Like Haydn, Mozart enjoyed a laugh, and his vibrant wit is often apparent in his music—especially in his *Musical Joke* K522, which lampoons lesser composers and inadequate performers. In private, however, his humor was less refined: the Mozart family is known to have had a penchant for the scatological, and correspondence between Wolfgang and his father ranges from the uproarious to the downright disgusting.

A scene from *Idomeneo*, Mozart's first big operatic hit.

1717 In London, four guilds of Freemasons unite to form, in 1723, the Grand Lodge of England; from this, all recognized grand lodges will be derived.

1755 The *Connoisseur*, an English periodical, on rouge: "We are indebted to Spanish wool for many of our masculine ruddy countenances."

1778 French playwright Beaumarchais finishes his play *Le Mariage de Figaro*; it is seen as openly anti-aristocratic and will not be performed until 1784.

1756~1791

Mozart Goes Freelance
The Mature Mozart

The year 1782 was a turning point for Mozart. He had moved to Vienna, hoping for a well-paid job at court, but was making a reasonable living as a freelance composer and teacher. At last he was getting the success he deserved—not as a Wunderkind, *but as a serious and talented composer. He had also managed by the move to escape the avaricious clutches of his domineering father (to some extent at least), and was showing real signs of maturity. At this time he befriended Haydn, and seemed to be influenced by more than just his music. While in Mannheim Mozart had fallen in love with Aloysia Weber (a cousin of the composer Carl Maria), but she rejected his advances; in 1782, he married her sister Constanze.*

Mozart, self-employed composer—probably because nobody would hire him.

Mozart and the Masons

One of the side effects of the Enlightenment was a growing interest in freemasonry. The pseudoreligious mythology and proclamation of brotherly love appealed to Mozart, who became an enthusiastic member. The influence of freemasonry can be seen in much of his later music, overtly in the Masonic cantatas, but more cryptically in other works, especially *Zauberflöte*, which is crammed with allusions to Masonic ritual and ideals.

Vienna was Mozart's home for the rest of his life. He realized that he didn't need to take on a paid job with a wealthy patron, and established himself as one of the first truly independent composers. By playing the piano, publishing sonatas (for solo piano, and piano and violin), and the occasional opera commission, he lived pretty well. Between 1782 and 1786 he wrote 15 piano concertos including some of his finest works, giving him the opportunity to establish his name as both composer and pianist: but more

TO WATCH

Apart from the operas, which are a must, don't miss the set of six string quartets dedicated to Haydn, and the string quintets K515 and K516, or if you prefer orchestral music, the piano concertos K482, K488, and K595, and the last four symphonies, nos. 38 (the "Prague"), 39, 40, and 41 (the "Jupiter"). The clarinet concerto is lovely too, and the four horn concertos are good-humored stuff. In distinct contrast, there's the requiem, usually in a version completed by Mozart's pupil Süssmayr.

WORKS

1782 Italian composer and violinist Niccolò Paganini is born; he will make his début as a violin virtuoso in Genoa in 1793.

1788 Britain's first penal settlement is sited at Botany Bay in Australia; when it is moved to a neighboring area, it is renamed Sydney after the British home secretary.

1790 Swiss entrepreneur Jacop Schweppe and partners set up the world's first company producing carbonated drinks; Schweppe's soda water will be sold in pharmacies.

important to him was the set of six string quartets that he dedicated to Haydn. Written more for his own satisfaction than as moneymakers, these show the serious side of Mozart, and a complete mastery of the genre.

The last five years of his life were largely taken up with opera: *Le Nozze di Figaro* (*The Marriage of Figaro*), *Don Giovanni*, *Così fan Tutte*, and *Die Zauberflöte* (*The Magic Flute*), which took traditional Italian opera and German *Singspiel* to hitherto unimagined heights. But he still found time to write instrumental music—piano sonatas, violin sonatas, string quartets and quintets, concertos for various instruments, and his last four symphonies.

Although his operas were well received elsewhere, especially in Prague, his appeal as a pianist in Vienna was beginning to

Amadeus and the Salieri Myth

Let's get this straight once and for all: Peter Schaffer's play *Amadeus* is terrific, but entirely without foundation. Salieri didn't poison Mozart, out of jealousy or for any other reason. And he didn't commission the requiem to frighten Mozart—it was requested by a nobleman who wanted to pass it off as his own work. Okay?

wane, and Mozart was beginning to find himself in financial difficulties. He had a modest income from a part-time court appointment, but was relying on commissions to maintain his lifestyle. He was overworked and ill when he received a mysterious commission to write a requiem mass, and died, aged only 35, before he could complete it.

A scene from Mozart's *Die Entführung aus dem Serail*, which he wrote in 1782.

1773 English musical historian Dr. Charles Burney publishes *The Present State of Music* in Germany, the Netherlands, and the United Provinces.

1776 America's Declaration of Independence is drafted by Thomas Jefferson and carried by the Congress.

1804 Napoleon declares himself emperor; Beethoven tears up the pages of the symphony "Eroica" that was once dedicated to Bonaparte.

1770~1827

Angry Young Man
Beethoven, Part One

Ludwig van Beethoven, who had every reason to look sullen and preoccupied.

Beethoven's father didn't do him any favors. He was an overbearing alcoholic and a second-rate musician, and he bullied poor young Ludwig into practicing the piano in the hope that he would become another Mozart. Ludwig learned quickly, and certainly showed great talent, but all his father ever really achieved was to make this rather ungainly child's life a complete and utter misery. Beethoven senior didn't have the drive and business acumen of Leopold Mozart, so Ludwig remained in comparative obscurity, working as a deputy organist for his father's employer, the elector of Cologne, in Bonn.

In 1787, the elector sent him to Vienna, where it looked like he would start to make his name—but after a few weeks he had to return to Bonn to look after his two younger brothers; his mother had died, and his feckless father had drunk himself out of a job. He supported the family by playing violin in a theater orchestra and giving piano lessons, but after five years

Beethoven realized there was no future for him in Bonn. He moved to Vienna in 1792, with financial help from the elector, and stayed there for the rest of his life.

Beethoven had composed a little as a teenager, even getting some music published, but felt the need to study further if he was to succeed in the musical world. He took lessons from Haydn (who

"☆"

Handicapped—but not Disabled

Beethoven is rightly famous for triumphing despite his deafness, but was not the only one to do so—William Boyce and Bedřich Smetana also went deaf in later life but continued composing. Others, including Frederick Delius and Handel, lost their sight at the height of their careers, and Francesco Landini, Antonio de Cabezón, and Joaquín Rodrigo were blind from childhood.

recognized his abilities, but found him uncouth and uncooperative), Albrechtsberger (ditto), and Salieri, and at the same time built up a circle of admirers among the local aristocracy. At age 25, he gave his first public performance and published his first important pieces, three piano trios op.1 and three piano sonatas op. 2. Beethoven the composer had finally arrived.

The music of the early period (Beethoven's work falls stylistically into three distinct periods—unimaginatively known as early, middle, and late) is very much in the classical style of Haydn and Mozart, but already Beethoven showed his passionate temperament and disregard for convention. In the piano music in particular—the first three piano concertos,

Deafness

Beethoven first noticed a loss of hearing in about 1796. In 1802, it was diagnosed as incurable, and likely to worsen. This shattering news prompted him to write a will-like letter addressed to his brothers, which describes his despair very movingly. The document became known as the "Heiligenstadt Testament," after the village in which it was written.

and piano sonatas such as the *Pathétique* and the *Sonata quasi una fantasia* (the "Moonlight")—Beethoven felt most comfortable and able to expand the forms and expressive content.

Although often considered a revolutionary composer, the Beethoven of the early period is actually more evolutionary, gradually feeling his way within classical forms. But when he realized that problems he had with his hearing were permanent, Beethoven overcame his despair and embarked on a phase of furious and extraordinary activity.

A masked ball at the Congress of Vienna. Beethoven's symphony no. 7 was performed.

TO WATCH

WORKS

Early period Beethoven is best heard in the piano music, particularly the first three piano concertos, the *Pathétique* sonata op.13, and the piano sonata op. 26, but the first symphony and the septet op. 20 are also good examples of his emerging originality. And try to remember when listening to the joyful second symphony that it was written in the same year as the heart-rending Heiligenstadt Testament.

TO WATCH

WORKS

1770 English naturalist Joseph Banks records the first sighting of an aboriginal boomerang, "about 2½ feet long, in shape much resembling a scymeter."

1796–1807 Fonthill Abbey, designed by James Wyatt, is the most exotic of Gothic buildings—it will collapse in 1825.

1799 During Napoleon's Egyptian campaign, Bouchard, an engineer, discovers the Rosetta Stone, which will provide the key to deciphering hieroglyphics.

1770~1827

Heroic Beethoven
The Late Ludwig Van

As deafness set in, Beethoven became more irritable and unkempt in his everyday life, changing from angry young man to miserable old grump. His music, too, underwent a profound change: not only did he reject the respectability of classicism, developing his own deeply expressive and turbulent style, but also adopted a heroic tone, with an emphasis on triumph over adversity and the indomitability of the human spirit. This of course mirrored his own experience, but also summed up the atmosphere of the new century—revolutions were throwing out the old order, and ordinary citizens taking charge of their own destiny.

A copy of Beethoven's death mask—hero with laurels.

Beethoven's "middle period" shows a radical departure from classical thinking—he was not writing for the nobility or the church, but for himself. The third symphony, the "Eroica," with its original dedication to Napoleon abandoned in disgust when Bonaparte proclaimed himself emperor, set the tone for the next ten years' work. It is a massive piece, about three times as long as the conventional symphonies of the time,

full of drama and apparent disregard for harmonic and formal rules. It was a turning point not only for Beethoven but for musical history, ushering in the Romanticism of the nineteenth century.

The "Eroica" was followed by a further five symphonies and two piano concertos over the next ten years, each pushing the boundaries of musical expression and expanding the range of

Title page of the "Eroica" symphony, once dedicated to Napoleon.

1819 In *Die Welt als Wille und Vorstellung*, German philosopher Arthur Schopenhauer propounds pessimistic views; God, free will, and immortality are illusions.

1819 François-Louis Cailler manufactures the first commercial eating chocolate at Vevey in Switzerland.

1826 A Pennsylvania law prohibits slave owners from recapturing slaves who have escaped to a free state; this law will be overturned in 1842.

the orchestra. The piano sonatas and string quartets of this period were similarly groundbreaking. The middle period also saw the production of Beethoven's only opera, *Fidelio*, with a suitably revolutionary and triumphant libretto, for which he wrote four versions of the overture before he was finally satisfied.

WORKS TO WATCH

It's impossible to include everything you really **must** listen to, but try piano concertos 4 and 5, and the violin concerto. For middle-period chamber music, there are the "Razumovsky" quartets op. 59 and piano sonatas such as the "Waldstein" op. 53 and the "Appassionata" op. 57. But for the sublime there's no beating the late piano sonatas (especially op. 110 and op. 111), the ninth symphony, and the last string quartets.

WORKS TO WATCH

and includes the glorious "Choral" symphony, no. 9, and the *Missa Solemnis*, but the crowning glory lies in the intensely personal and spiritual late string quartets and piano sonatas. Although contemporary audiences (and indeed many modern ones) found them impossibly idiosyncratic, they are testimony of an extraordinary musical genius.

Beethoven's ear trumpet. As deafness deepened, he relied on his fantastic musical imagination.

This period of prolific creativity came to an abrupt end in 1812. Beethoven was so deaf that he could no longer perform in public (he conducted a charity concert in 1814, but couldn't even hear the rapturous applause). He was also disappointed in love, had a legal battle for custody of his late brother's son, and not surprisingly fell into deep depression. But somehow he dragged himself out of these "silent" years and started composing again.

Now completely isolated from outside influences by total deafness, Beethoven was forced into originality, and sought his inspiration from deep within. His late period kicks off with the massive "Hammerklavier" piano sonata op. 106,

Notebooks

Beethoven seldom composed at the keyboard, preferring to work at his desk or making notes as he walked around. His notebooks are full of almost illegible jottings and reworkings which give an insight into the way he constantly revised his work. He also used notepads to hold conversations as he got deafer, which make really fascinating reading.

1795 Scottish explorer Mungo Park investigates West Africa and the Niger River.

1798 Prague-born Munich actor-playwright Aloys Senefelder invents lithography; ink impressions are taken from a flat stone covered with a greasy substance.

1804 Charles Ledoux designs his Chaux Ideal City, in which some buildings are spherical or cylindrical; it is never built.

1797~1828

Take Me to Your Lieder
Cue for a Song

As a sort of coda to the trio of great Viennese classical composers, the next generation produced Franz SCHUBERT (1797–1828). Unlike Haydn, Mozart, and Beethoven, Schubert was Viennese by birth, and he lived in his hometown for the whole of his tragically short life. Although he wasn't a great innovator, his phenomenal gift for melody writing and meticulous craftsmanship assure him a place among the all-time greats.

Franz Schubert was a popular guest at private parties hosted by the middle class of Vienna, performing his latest pieces on the piano.

Party Time

Most of Schubert's music was never publicly performed until after his death, but in his lifetime he was well known by the Viennese middle-class intelligentsia for being the life and soul of their soirées. Much of his piano and chamber music, and of course his songs, were performed regularly at these get-togethers, which later acquired the nickname "Schubertiads."

Schubert started composing as a schoolboy at the imperial court chapel, where his teachers included Salieri, and by the time he left in 1813 he had already written an impressive number of pieces. After school, he went back to live with his father and stepmother and ended up as a schoolteacher, just like his dad. Well, not quite . . . Schubert senior was modestly successful as a teacher, but Franz was hopeless. And he found that teaching got in the way of composing

1806–8 Ludwig Joachim von Arnim and Clemens Maria Brentano publish a collection of German folksongs, *Des Knaben Wunderhorn.*

1824 Quaker John Cadbury opens a tea and coffee shop in Birmingham, England; he will experiment with sugar and powdered chocolate.

1836 Danish businessman Christian Thomsen classifies ancient Scandinavian artifacts by material and use and devises the "Three-Age System."

(although you'd hardly know it: during three years' teaching he wrote four masses, five symphonies, the odd string quartet, an opera, and literally hundreds of *Lieder*— German for "songs"—including some of his most famous, such as "Gretchen am Spinnrade" and "Erlkönig"), so he decided in 1816 to take up composing full-time.

When Schubert left the school, he shared an apartment with a law student and started to mix in literary and artistic circles. His new friends were enormously appreciative of his music and regularly got together for private performances of his songs, with the composer at the piano. He was the toast of the middle classes in Vienna but wasn't getting any of his music publicly performed, let alone published, so found life difficult financially. He had the occasional commission, such as for the "Trout" quintet, and a brief teaching job at Esterháza, but didn't enjoy the luxury of a salary from a rich patron.

UNFINISHED BUSINESS

Undaunted, Schubert carried on composing, not only *Lieder* but also operas (none of which achieved any success). By the mid-1820s he had perfected his individual lyrical style, producing symphony no. 8 (the "Unfinished"), the song cycle *Die schöne Müllerin*, and the string quartets in A minor and D minor ("Death and the Maiden"). In his final years, when syphilis and typhoid were setting in, he surpassed even these achievements with a final symphony (the "Great" C major), the string quartet in G, piano sonata in B flat, and the *Winterreise* song cycle—all triumphs.

Schubert's admirers—known as Schubertinis— organized such events as musical outings to the country in celebration of their hero.

1800 In Europe, magic lanterns (optical projectors) are equipped with "limelights," which use quicklime to produce a glow.

1800 In England, sheep theft, sodomy, murder, impersonating an army veteran, and stealing an article worth more than 5 shillings are capital offenses.

1815 Learning of Napoleon's defeat at Waterloo, banker Nathan Rothschild buys British government stocks and makes a financial killing.

1800~1900

Man, I'm Really Expressing Myself

Romanticism: An Overview

First Mozart, and then Beethoven and Schubert—pretty soon everybody was going it alone, giving up the security of patronage for the relative freedom of composing what they wanted. The idea that music should be in praise of God, or a respectable entertainment for the aristocracy, had been replaced by composition as a means of self-expression. Composers and performers were expected by their adoring middle-class audiences to be bohemian and eccentric; even the hairstyles had changed from powdered wigs to unkempt and straggling locks. The nineteenth century had arrived, and with it the age of Romanticism.

The Concert Overture and Symphonic Poem

A new genre of orchestral work appeared in the nineteenth century, a one-movement piece of program music, usually in sonata form. At first it was known as the "concert overture" because of its similarities to opera overtures, although it wasn't an overture *to* anything, but rather a self-contained item. Then along came Franz Liszt, who wrote a few himself and decided to call them "symphonic poems." Same meat, different gravy.

Young Franz Liszt, epitome of the Romantic performer and composer.

Several things differentiate Romantic music from the classical models from which it evolved. Most obviously, it is more overtly emotional, and less concerned with form and balance; the forms created and polished by Haydn and Mozart were no longer seen as ends in themselves, but as convenient vehicles for the outpourings of the Romantic soul.

PROGRAM NOTES

The Romantic movement was something of a reaction to the Enlightenment ideals of reason, elegance, and civilization, and had its beginnings in the *Sturm und Drang* of late eighteenth-century German literature. Romantic music had a lot in common with the literature of the period, especially its preoccupation with the power of Nature, the occult, and "Gothic," and emphasis on emotional extremes—often fueled by

1823 Up until this date in England, all suicides are required by law to be buried at a crossroads with a stake through the heart.

1826 The English Parliament introduces imperial weights and measures, abandoning the Anglo-Saxon quartern, hogshead, and furlong.

1890s British inspector general of the Bengali police, Edward Henry, introduces the fingerprinting of criminals; he will become known as Mr. Fingertips.

opium or laudanum. Because of these literary connections, much of the music of the period was "program music"—instrumental music that tells a story or depicts a particular scene—and these pieces often had descriptive titles.

In the quest for ever more expressive music, the Romantics extended their harmonic language, using more and more exotic chords and dramatic changes of key, a progression that led to the eventual breakdown of the whole system. They also explored the coloristic possibilities of various instruments. The orchestra was growing steadily, to include larger numbers of brass, woodwind, and percussion instruments; composers had a larger palette of different timbres than ever before at their disposal. Orchestration, the art of effectively combining or contrasting the various tone colors of the orchestra, became an integral part of composition.

Faust in his study, considering the wisdom of his deal with Mephistopheles.

Faust and the Romantics

Recurrent themes in Romantic program music were death, the supernatural, Satan, sex, and man versus the elements. Luckily, one of the heroes of the Romantic movement, the poet Johann Wolfgang von Goethe (1749–1832), managed to write a play incorporating all of these—*Faust*. It inspired dozens of compositions, notably Gounod's opera *Faust*, Berlioz's *La Damnation de Faust*, Liszt's *Faust Symphony*, Schumann's *Scenes from Goethe's Faust,* and Wagner's *A Faust Overture*.

The piano also came into its own in the nineteenth century. With its wide dynamic range, it was ideally suited to Romantic music, and virtuoso pianist-composers (and the odd violinist) toured the world showing off their skills and baring their tortured souls to ecstatic and adoring audiences. This phenomenon was the birth of the piano recital as a star event. All in all, a far cry from the restrained world of elegant classicism and the respectable aristocratic courts of only a generation or so before.

Digression

Tools of the Trade

The violin, highest of strings, and backbone of the orchestra.

By the mid–nineteenth century, the orchestra was the cornerstone of classical music (in its broader sense), and had become the full "symphony orchestra" we see today. From the fatal staff-wielding of Lully in front of his "24 violins" had evolved a baton-waving conductor and mighty ensemble of strings, woodwinds, brass, percussion, and more.

The basis of any orchestra, however, is the string section (without it the ensemble is simply a "band"), subdivided into five groups. There are usually two groups of violins (first violins and second violins—what else?), the highest sounding of the family, and a group each (getting progressively lower) of violas, cellos, and double basses. Altogether, there are generally 50–60 players in the modern string section.

Next, there's the woodwind section, usually arranged behind the strings in pairs or groups of three of each instrument. At the top are the flutes, or even their smaller version, the piccolo, below which are clarinets, oboes, and finally, bassoons. Occasional visitors to this section include saxophones, bass clarinets, the cor anglais (a sort of big brother to the oboe), and lowest of the low, the contrabassoon.

Behind them sit the brass, ranging from the highest, the three trumpets, down through the four horns and three trombones to the solitary tuba. And finally, at the back of the stage, there's an array of hardware known as the

percussion section, which as well as the familiar timpani or kettledrums boasts all kinds of drums, cymbals, gongs, triangles, xylophones, bells, rattles, and even sirens.

As if that wasn't enough, some composers include parts for piano, harp, organ, guitar, mandolin, synthesizer, or whatever . . .

The Italian for bassoon, *fagotto*, means "bundle of sticks."

CHAMBER GROUPS

Of course, these instruments don't appear only in an orchestral setting. Chamber groups, ensembles of up to about nine players, can have any combination of them. The string groups you're most likely to come across are the string trio (violin, viola, cello) and string quartet (two violins, viola, cello), although there are also larger string ensembles.

Timpani were often the only percussion instruments in early orchestras.

Sometimes an instrument from a different family is added to the strings to form, for example, a piano trio (piano, violin, cello), piano quartet (piano, violin, viola, cello), or even a clarinet quintet (clarinet plus string quartet). Occasionally you'll find groups of wind players too, most often in a wind quintet (flute, oboe, clarinet, horn, and bassoon).

CHOIRS AND VOICES

Basically, there are four categories of voice: soprano, alto, tenor, and bass. But it's a bit more complicated than that. Female singers are either soprano (with high voices) or contralto (low voices, usually abbreviated to "alto"), although there are some who fall between the two, called mezzo-soprano. Similarly, the male voices are either tenor (high) or bass (low), or somewhere in between (baritone), or even above (alto—confusing, huh?). Then there are boys whose voices haven't broken (trebles) and, until the end of the nineteenth century, castrati (whose voices never broke), as well as counter-tenors, men who sing "falsetto," which is a weird emulation of castrato singing. Most choirs stick to a four-voice format.

A full modern symphony orchestra prepares to take a bow.

1803 The music prize, the Prix de Rome, is awarded for the first time in France.

1805 A Japanese surgeon performs the first known surgical operation using an anesthetic.

1825 The New York Stock Exchange opens; most of the securities will be shares in canal, turnpike, mining, and gaslighting companies.

1800~1850
How Romantic!
Early Romantics

Although Schubert's music was inspired by Romantic ideas, it was classical in structure and conception; likewise, Beethoven can't be seen as a true Romantic— even his late period works are formally rooted in the eighteenth-century tradition. While these two Viennese giants were at the height of their creative powers, the first of the German Romantics was working on an opera that contained all the elements of the new style.

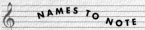
NAMES TO NOTE

*Other early Romantics you might come across are **Louis Spohr** (1784–1859), who wrote some tuneful chamber music as well as numerous other works, and **Carl Czerny** (1791–1857), and if you're very lucky **Clara Schumann** (née Wieck) (1819–96). She gave up a promising career as a composer to promote her husband's music, but a few of her compositions have survived (better than Robert, some say . . .).*

C*arl Maria von Weber* (1786–1826) finished his opera *Der Freischütz* (*The Freeshooter*) in 1820, and it was first performed a year later. The subject matter

was typically Romantic, involving the supernatural, the Devil, dreams, awe-inspiring Nature, and plenty of the usual hunting and drinking songs; it was also German in both language and sentiment, breaking once and for all the hold Italian opera had on the rest of the world. And the musical language was quite different too. The structure is determined by dramatic and psychological demands rather than by abstract forms, and it uses extremes of orchestration and harmony for even greater, more impressive emotional impact. Weber was the first great Romantic composer, even dying of that most Romantic disease, consumption.

Clara Schumann accompanying a violinist. She was recognized as a talented pianist and composer, but, alas, only a woman.

1825 George Stephenson's pioneer steam engine, *Locomotion*, transports 300 people and 12 coal wagons from Shildon colliery to Stockton.

1830 French novelist Stendhal (Marie-Henri Beyle) publishes *Le Rouge et le noir*, charting the rise and fall of a Romantic hero.

1850 Bavarian-American entrepreneur Levi Strauss, learning that California miners need hard-wearing trousers, makes up and successfully markets "bibless overalls."

In contrast, *Felix* MENDELSSOHN-BARTHOLDY (1809–47) had a very different attitude to the Romantic. Where Weber saw Nature as awesome, Mendelssohn found it magnificent; Weber was preoccupied with the darkly supernatural, while Mendelssohn seems to have been obsessed by fairies. And Weber was quintessentially German, while Mendelssohn was cosmopolitan, and traveled widely. Consequently his musical style is lighter, as in the symphonies inspired by his trips to Scotland and Italy, and the famous *Hebrides* overture ("Fingal's Cave"). Even when selecting a Shakespearean subject for his music he avoided the tragedies in favor of *A Midsummer Night's Dream*.

For the archetypical Romantic, though, look no further than *Robert* SCHUMANN (1810–56).

He had everything going for him—a literary background, unrequited love, syphilis, a concert career wrecked by a hand injury, and finally, insanity.

Robert Schumann.

Weber is principally known for opera, but some instrumental pieces get played occasionally—the *Konzertstück* for piano and orchestra, and *Aufforderung zum Tanz*. With Mendelssohn there's more choice: orchestral music such as the *Hebrides* overture, incidental music for *A Midsummer Night's Dream*, symphonies nos. 3, the "Scottish," and 4, the "Italian," and the violin concerto; or the oratorio *Elijah*, and the *Songs Without Words* for piano. Schumann's most characteristic music is in the piano works, such as *Carnaval* and *Kinderszenen*, or the song cycles *Dichterliebe* and *Frauenliebe und -Leben*, but symphonies 1, "Spring," and 3, "Rhenish," and the piano concerto are also worth a listen.

Weber's "Invitation to the Dance," one of his lighter pieces, was a hit in the 1820s, just before the waltzes of the Strauss family.

Schumann had a long legal battle to get his piano teacher's consent to marry his daughter, Clara Wieck, but managed only a few years' wedded bliss before depression set in. After a suicide attempt in 1854, he admitted himself to an asylum, where he died a couple of years later. Nevertheless, before his breakdown he wrote some fine music. His early works are mainly for the piano, and often have literary allusions or cryptogramic ideas—the *Abegg Variations*, for instance, use the notes A-B-E-G-G— but after his marriage he turned to song and later still orchestral music.

1800 German writer, composer, music critic, and illustrator Ernst Hoffmann's *Tales* combine fantasy and magic and will inspire Offenbach's *Tales of Hoffmann*.

1852 At a Connecticut séance, 19-year-old medium Daniel D. Home is unexpectedly "taken up in the air... and...carried to the ceiling of the apartment."

1858 Unusually hot, dry weather causes a sharp fall in the Thames River in London; "the Great Stink" precipitates the development of sewage disposal.

1800~1880
Brilliant!
The Virtuosi

Arch-Romantic Chopin composing at the piano, with a doting fan.

The public concert was a well-established part of cultural life by the nineteenth century, and several composers had already made their names by performing their own music. But with Romanticism and its obsession with expressing extremes of emotion came a new breed of composer-performer: the angst-ridden virtuoso of questionable moral rectitude who could strut his stuff in front of adoring, often predominantly female audiences. These boys became the international pop idols of their day, commanding huge fees and playing concertos and solo recitals to packed houses.

The Waltz
A new dance craze swept across Europe from 1830s Vienna. Johann Strauss the elder (1804–49) and his two sons Johann (1825–99) and Josef (1827–70) were largely responsible for the waltz's popularity, but even "serious" composers such as Brahms, Chopin, and Ravel succumbed to its charms. Not everybody was so enthusiastic: it was condemned as immoral because of the close proximity of the dancing partners, and unhealthy because of their speed of movement.

The first of these to make it big was *Niccolò PAGANINI* (1782–1840), an extraordinarily gifted violinist (and, unusually for the time, guitarist). There wasn't a great deal of suitable music so he wrote his own pieces, using all kinds of tricks to dazzle the audience with his technical ability. He spent most of his life on tour throughout Europe, and died a wealthy (but exhausted) man. He paved the way for the next generation of virtuosi, but it has to be said that his music, although spectacular, wasn't exactly profound.

But *Frédéric* (originally Fryderyk Franciszek) *CHOPIN* (1810–49) was a different kettle of fish. Son of a French

1861 The "Battle Hymn of the Republic," with lyrics by Julia Ward Howe and set to the tune of "Glory Glory Hallelujah," appears in the *Atlantic Monthly*.

1872 Charles Darwin's *The Expressions of the Emotions in Man and Animals* reports: "with English women, blushing does not extend to the neck and upper part of the chest."

1868 American John Wesley Hyatt invents celluloid and wins a competition to find a cheap replacement for ivory billiard balls.

Old Nick

Because of his sinister appearance, remote manner, bohemian lifestyle, and superhuman virtuosity on the violin, Niccolò Paganini was often seen as a man possessed. Literally. A rumor went around that he was in league with the Devil, and there was even some serious discussion as to whether he was Satan himself. Honest.

schoolmaster and Polish mother, he was brought up in Warsaw, but soon toured Europe giving concerts, eventually settling in Paris in 1831.

Chopin was idolized not so much for his technical brilliance but for his sensitive playing and expressive compositions. These were almost exclusively for solo piano, structurally conventional, but using harmony in a completely new way. Less of a showman than Paganini, Chopin was more Romantic in both his music and his lifestyle; his many affairs included a notorious liaison with George Sand, and he died, Romantically, of consumption.

If you were a virtuoso pianist, Paris seemed the place to be in the mid-nineteenth century. Among the many pianist-composers there were the startlingly original American *Louis Moreau Gottschalk* (1829–69) and, most famous of all the showmen, the Hungarian *Franz* (originally Ferenc) *Liszt* (1811–86). Liszt had it all: Paganini's bravura stage manner

and sparkling virtuosity, and Chopin's sensitivity and compositional ability. The public adored it and lapped it up— Europe was swamped by what was known as "Lisztomania" (and you thought all that stuff about groupies started in the 1960s).

At first Chopin concentrated on works for solo piano, but, as his confidence grew, branched out into orchestral works, often on a massive scale. A lurid private life was *de rigueur* for the Romantic virtuoso, and Liszt was no exception, but in retirement he took holy orders.

TO WATCH

WORKS

Paganini was more a performer than a composer, but the 24 *Caprices* op.1, and the 2d and 3d violin concertos, are more than just showpieces. Chopin, however, seldom wrote a bad piece— try any of the nocturnes, polonaises, waltzes, and études, and you're in for a treat. And Liszt? All good bravura stuff, especially the *Hungarian Rhapsodies* for piano, the piano sonata, and orchestral pieces such as the *Faust* and *Dante* symphonies.

TO WATCH

WORKS

Liszt plays the piano to an audience of famous names, under the watchful bust of Beethoven.

1821 Hector Berlioz, medical student, visits the dissecting room at the Hospice de la Pitié and sees "fragments of limbs, the grinning faces and gaping skulls."

1868 Secondo Pia photographs the Turin shroud and discovers the negative image of a face and mutilated body, believed to be that of the crucified Christ.

1872 The brigantine *Mary Celeste* sets sail from New York to Genoa; the abandoned ship is sighted a month later in the Azores but none of her crew is ever found.

1803–1869

Fantastic!

Berlioz

With composers such as Chopin and Liszt, the piano had become central to musical Romanticism, and Paris was becoming a center for composers and virtuosi from all over the world. But there seemed to be no home-grown talent in France, where the musical establishment was notoriously conservative, at least until the appearance of Hector BERLIOZ (1803–69). Not only was he a lone Frenchman in a world dominated by German and Eastern European composers, but he also suffered a severe disadvantage for a musician of the period—he was a lousy pianist.

"A Witches' Sabbath"—the chilling climax of the *Symphonie fantastique*.

TO WATCH

WORKS

Don't miss the *Symphonie fantastique*, but look out also for *Harold en Italie*, a symphony with a solo viola part, and the concert overtures *Les Francs-juges, Carnaval romain*, and *Le Corsaire*—stunning! There are also overtures to the three operas, *Benvenuto Cellini, Les Troyens*, and *Béatrice et Bénédict*, if you can't face the full works. For choral music on a grand scale there's the *Grande messe des morts* and *La Damnation de Faust*. Fantastic stuff!

TO WATCH

WORKS

Undeterred by this shortcoming, Berlioz played on his strengths and composed in the idioms he knew best: orchestral and vocal music. In a way, he was filling a gap that had appeared in the repertoire with all that piano music stealing the show, and carrying on the tradition of symphonic writing. As a young man he had been bowled over by Beethoven's symphonies, and saw them as his starting point.

His first major work was the amazing *Symphonie fantastique* of 1830, a five-movement symphony bearing all the hallmarks of his style. Berlioz was well read, and especially loved Shakespeare, Goethe, and Byron, but was also an

1879 British chemist Alfred Bird's obituary describes his skill at playing "a beautiful set of harmonized glass bowls" but not his invention of Bird's custard.

1883 The island of Krakatoa is destroyed by a series of volcanic eruptions; 40,000 people die and the sound reverberates in Australia and Singapore.

1884 The safety bicycle has pneumatic tires, medium-sized wheels, chain linkage, adjustable handlebars, a cushioned seat, and brakes.

" ☆ "

Writings

Berlioz also wrote several books, including a treatise on orchestration. More entertaining, though, are his *Mémoires*, a hugely exaggerated account of his life and loves, written in a sort of literary equivalent to his subjective and colorful musical language.

obsessive and melodramatic character. He fell passionately in love with the actress Harriet Smithson after seeing her playing Ophelia, declared his undying love, and despite her rejection wrote the *Symphonie fantastique* to try to win her over. The symphony tells the story of unrequited and obsessive love, drug-induced dreams of guillotines, and witches' sabbaths, in some of the most dramatic music ever written—Berlioz's orchestration and harmony are breathtaking. He also uses a device frequently employed by later composers for dramatic and formal coherence, the recurrent theme, the *idée fixe*, which represents the object of his desires. (Oh, and he got the girl eventually, married her in 1833, but they separated in 1842.)

A colorful character from *Benvenuto Cellini*.

Berlioz's use of the orchestra wasn't always fully appreciated.

A difficult act to follow, that, but he went on to write further programmatic symphonies and concert overtures, all with literary allusions, and also several operas, but never really got the recognition he deserved during his lifetime. Nor the money, although he made some extra cash as a music critic, and Paganini commissioned the *Harold en Italie* symphony and sent him money so he could carry on with his work. He died a lonely and disheartened man, and it was almost a century before he was fully appreciated.

Big Bands

To audiences that had found Beethoven's symphonies ear-shattering, the sheer size of the orchestra Berlioz used must have been overwhelming. He wrote for massive orchestral forces, creating a sound that inspired Liszt to try his hand too, and starting a trend for ever-expanding orchestras that continued through the nineteenth century.

1832 Just before his death, Johann Wolfgang von Goethe completes Part II of his drama *Faust*; it is a masterpiece of German literature and an inspiration to composers.

1834 English farm laborers, the Tolpuddle "martyrs," trying to maintain meager wages, are sentenced to transportation for trade-union activities in Dorset.

1857 Philip Gosse publishes *Omphalos*, a vain attempt to—as his son Edmund Gosse would later write— "fling geology into the arms of Scripture."

1833~1897

A Classical Romantic

Brahms

Just as Schubert is sometimes described as a "Romantic Classicist," pouring Romantic ideas into essentially classical forms, so Johannes BRAHMS (1833–97) can be looked on as a "Classical Romantic," striving for a classical formality in Romantic idioms. A reserved and scholarly man, a rather conservative and academic composer, and an outspoken critic of Liszt's musical excesses, Brahms was something of an anachronism. Nevertheless, his music was of high quality and emotional depth, and he had quite a following; music lovers were classified at the time as followers of either Brahms, or Liszt and Wagner.

Brahms enjoying a cigar and a walk to his favorite inn, The Red Hedgehog.

Compared with many other composers, Brahms was a rather late starter, or at least a slow developer. Although he had done some composing and arranging as a teenager, it wasn't until 1853, when he went on a concert tour with the violinist Reményi, that he took up composition seriously. On tour, he met Liszt, and also the conductor and violinist Joseph Joachim, who suggested he should introduce himself to Schumann, a meeting which had a profound effect (see boxes). Schumann immediately recognized Brahms's talent and encouraged him to follow a career in composition.

For Brahms, who was a well-brought-up lad, this meant getting a respectable job, not freelancing like the disreputable Liszt and Chopin. Unfortunately, he couldn't get a post of any real importance, and ended up teaching

" ☆ "

What the Critics Said

Robert Schumann was especially fulsome in his praise of Brahms, hailing him as a genius in the *Neue Zeitschrift für Musik*, but many critics found him too dry and academic. Tchaikovsky went further, referring in his diary to "...that scoundrel Brahms. What a giftless bastard!" There's nothing like constructive criticism. Nowadays we hear considerable passion concealed behind the formal exterior of Brahms's music.

1873 A missionary in China is instructed in Feng Shui; "It's a thing like wind which you cannot comprehend, and like water which you cannot grasp."

1890s The British invent an indoor version of lawn tennis, for rainy days; under the trademark Ping-Pong, it will achieve international popularity.

1891 The first Cruft's dog show is staged by Charles Cruft in Britain; Cruft's will become an internationally famous annual event.

TO WATCH

WORKS

Key works in Brahms's career are the *German Requiem* and the four symphonies, but there's a lot more besides. Try the two piano concertos and the violin concerto, and the wonderfully inventive *Variations on a Theme by Haydn*. He could be just as ingenious and expressive on a small scale too, and wrote a good deal of chamber music, notably the three string quartets and the clarinet quintet, and songs, including the deeply moving *Vier ernste Gesänge.*

TO WATCH

WORKS

and conducting minor ensembles: it wasn't until he performed his first piano concerto in 1859 that he was noticed by the public. Being of a classical turn of mind, he was attracted to Vienna, and was briefly director of the *Singakademie* there. He devoted himself full time to composition from about 1864, concentrating mainly on his next major work, the *German Requiem*, which was to secure his reputation.

BEETHOVEN'S TENTH

Brahms had also been working, on and off since 1855, on a symphony. The success of the *German Requiem* and the *Variations on the St. Anthony Chorale* in the 1870s encouraged him to complete it (I did say he was a slow developer). It was finished in 1876 and hailed as a worthy

successor to Beethoven's symphonies, spurring Brahms on to a positive flurry of composition (for him at least) over the next ten years. He followed up the first symphony with another three, a second piano concerto, a violin concerto, and also wrote a fair number of songs and chamber pieces. In his mid-fifties he decided to retire, but in the case of Brahms this meant writing small-scale pieces, which he continued to do, producing many gems until shortly before his death.

Johannes Brahms—a dry old stick with hidden depths.

Clara and Johannes

Brahms visited the Schumanns in 1853. He impressed Robert greatly, and apparently Clara made a deep impression on him. Schumann was admitted to an asylum a few months after his first meeting with Brahms, who dropped everything to help Clara and her children. He was obviously smitten with her, and she in turn dependent on him, but even after Robert died they lived apart, and probably remained celibately, though remained in touch for the rest of their lives.

The object of Brahms's devotions, Clara Schumann, in about 1875.

1818-31 The city of Turin is replanned; wide streets and large squares are flanked by arcaded buildings in the tradition of the seventeenth-century style.

1872 Having traveled widely in rural America, Aaron Montgomery Ward thinks up the sales catalogue; by 1895, his illustrated catalogue will be in more homes than the Bible.

1884 Sicilian novelist Giovanni Verga adapts his short story into a play, *Cavalleria Rusticana*, which will provide the basis for Pietro Mascagni's opera.

1800–1924

A Night at the Opera
Nineteenth-Century Italy

The Romantic movement was very much a Germanic thing, and the nineteenth century saw northern European composers overtly expressing their emotions in music for the first time. After all that repression, it manifested itself in dramatically angst-ridden, Gothic stuff a lot of the time. The Italians couldn't care less about all that—they had been musically extroverted for centuries, and didn't really understand what all the fuss was about. To them, the nineteenth century was just an extension of previous styles, and in Italy that meant only one thing: opera.

Gioachino Rossini trying in vain to disguise the bulge in his waistcoat.

Offenbach
While Vienna had the Strauss family as an antidote to all that heavy Germanic romanticism, France's counterbalance to Berlioz was the German-born Parisian Jacques Offenbach (1819–80). Like the Strausses, he was a skillful composer and did a lot to establish light opera and musical comedy as a respectable genre. Look out for *Orphée aux enfers* (with its famous cancan), *La Vie parisienne*, and *Les Contes d'Hoffmann*. As much a part of *la gaieté parisienne* as Toulouse-Lautrec, and as Gallic as absinthe.

And at the beginning of the century, that meant only one composer—*Gioachino ROSSINI* (1792–1868). He wrote dozens of operas, both comic (they're genuinely funny) and serious, to international acclaim, ignoring all the modern ideas of Weber and the like and going his own sweet way in an essentially classical style. His greatest hits were *The Barber of Seville* (first performed in 1816) and *William Tell* (1829), but all his work shows a mastery of the genre. Sensibly, he decided to rest on his laurels after *William Tell*, before he could be accused of being old-fashioned; he had enough money to enjoy a lengthy retirement, turning out the odd masterpiece like the *Petite messe solenelle*.

> ### " ⭐ "
> #### Rossini and Food
> When Rossini retired, he decided to devote himself to his second great love, food. He was an enthusiastic cook and a voracious gourmet—as can be seen by the lack of waistline in paintings of him. His name is immortalized as much in the *Tournedos Rossini* as the *William Tell* overture.

1911 Italian-born car maker Ettore Bugatti's eight-valve, four-cylinder Bugatti car wins in its category at the Grand Prix du Mans; he will dominate car racing for 20 years.

1915 Italy declares war on her former ally Austria in the hope of gaining territory; Italian offensives will produce no gains and 250,000 casualties.

1917 Composer Victor Herbert successfully sues Shanley's Café in New York for using his songs without permission.

Although only slightly younger than Rossini, *Gaetano DONIZETTI* (1797–1848) and *Vincenzo BELLINI* (1801–35) belonged to the next generation of opera composers. Their work only came to public notice after Rossini had retired, and was more Romantic in spirit, on a larger scale, and more dramatic. Bellini had all the right Romantic credentials, too, living a tragically short and immoral life, and Donizetti died of syphilis.

THE FORCE OF DESTINY

Next in line, and the greatest of the lot, came *Giuseppe VERDI* (1813–1901). Other than a string quartet, the dramatic *Requiem*, and a few other pieces, his output was exclusively operatic. He made his name with *Rigoletto*, *Il Trovatore*, and *La Traviata* in the 1850s, building on Donizetti's dramatic style and showing an amazing breadth of expression. His musical language

A distraught Rodolfo

A consumptive Mimi

A concerned Marcello

A distraught Rodolfo and concerned Marcello discuss Mimi's health in Puccini's *La Bohème*.

Another nineteenth-century Italian to look out for is **Amilcare Ponchielli** *(1834–86), but these days you're only likely to hear the "Dance of the Hours" from his opera* La Gioconda *(brilliantly desecrated in Disney's* Fantasia*). And although he doesn't belong chronologically here, mention must be made of* **Ottorino Respighi** *(1879–1936), whose orchestral works, especially* Fontane di Roma, Pini di Roma, *and* Feste Romane, *are very much in the late Romantic style.*

The cover of a piano transcription of *Rigoletto*, Verdi's masterpiece of violent passion.

Rigoletto the hunchbacked jester

Gilda, the doomed heroine

The wicked Duke

expanded with operas such as *Aïda*, *Otello*, and *Falstaff*, and he never gave up the "set pieces," the arias, and ensembles, for the sake of dramatic realism. The move to operatic *verismo*, realism, was made by his natural successor *Giacomo PUCCINI* (1858–1924) in *Tosca*, which he followed with truly romantic operas such as *Madama Butterfly* and *Turandot*.

1816 The waltz comes to the U.S.; critics see it "as the only really deadly sin—worse than Perjury, and scarcely equaled by malicious Homicide."

1818 At Angostura in Venezuela, German physician Johann Siegert prepares a stomach tonic from gentian root and rum; Angostura bitters will be widely used in "pink gin."

1840 Robert Schumann marries Clara Wieck despite her father's strenuous opposition; this year he will compose *Dichterliebe* and *Frauenliebe und -Leben.*

1813~1883

All Night at the Opera
Wagner

Richard Wagner.

For some, Verdi is the opera composer. For others it's Puccini. But for this book, because of the effect his musical language had, it's got to be Richard WAGNER (1813–83). You'll probably detest the man, and you'll either love or hate his music, but you can't be indifferent to him. Just about every composer since Wagner has been influenced directly or indirectly by his music, as often as not by reacting against it. Single-handedly, he changed the course of musical history. That's why he gets two pages to himself, even though he wrote almost nothing but opera.

So what did he do that was so dramatic? Well, for a start he saw opera (he preferred the term "music drama") as a complete artwork, combining theater and music in a continuous narrative, rather than tedious recitative interrupted by pretty arias. Singers were seen as actors who sang parts essential to the plot, not just to show off their vocal pyrotechnics. Above all he stressed realism—which, let's face it, you don't see much in Baroque and classical opera. This idea was really only taking Weber's conception of opera one stage further, but totally went against the original, and very artificial, Italian model.

A Small Town in Germany

Not content to have his operas performed in the all-purpose opera houses, Wagner had a festival theater built in Bayreuth, Bavaria, devoted exclusively to his own work, and directed by members of his family since his death. Dedicated fans make an annual pilgrimage to the summer Wagner Festival there, like Moslems to Mecca. Don't confuse it with Beirut.

Scenery for *Tristan und Isolde,* the beginning of the end for tonality, and still considered one of the most intense and sustained experiences in all Western music.

1874 British missionaries describe trepanning operations practiced by Pacific Islanders—eight out of ten patients recover.

1879 "Toros, toros!" A little Spanish girl discovers cave paintings in Altamira; the work of Cro-Magnon man, they date back some 30,000 years.

1888 Professor Flinders Petrie discovers the foundations of the world's largest known labyrinth, built by Egyptian king Amenemhet III c.2000 BC.

But it's the musical language that concerns us here. Wagner's operas are like huge programmatic symphonies—but long, *really* long—and his style has more in common with Romantic instrumental style. The orchestra wasn't just an accompaniment to the singers but an integral part of the action, using every instrument available to him (plus a few of his own invention) for dramatic effect. The only orchestrator to match him was Berlioz.

WORKS TO WATCH

Rossini famously remarked, "Wagner has good moments, but dreadful quarter-hours," and it's true the operas are a bit of a marathon. Plenty of excerpts are played as concert items, such as *The Flying Dutchman* and *Die Meistersinger* overtures, and the *Ride of the Valkyries*. But if you can face it, try one of the complete operas—you might just end up a fan.

WORKS TO WATCH

WITH THIS RING

Remember the *idée fixe* in Berlioz's *Symphonie fantastique*? Well, Wagner did the same sort of thing in his four-opera cycle *Der Ring des Nibelungen*, with what he called a *Leitmotiv* (leading motif): different musical figures reappear in various guises in the operas, representing characters as well as scenes or even moods.

But Wagner's most significant innovations were harmonic. For centuries composers had used dramatic key changes, the occasional chromatic chord, and dissonances for expressive effect; Wagner rocked the boat by using these devices almost continuously. The effect is disorienting, undermining the basis of the system of tonality (music in specific keys), and provoking a crisis in musical thinking.

DIE WALKÜRE.
Sigmund's Tod.

Wagner at his most Wagnerian, the death of Sigmund in *Die Walküre*.

Ego and Superego

Wagner was good. Very good. And boy, did he know it. If there were prizes for the most arrogant, self-obsessed, or opinionated composer, he would win them hands down. He was also intolerant, especially of composers he thought lesser in stature than himself (which meant everyone), and rabidly anti-Semitic. Shame, he wrote such good stuff.

1880 British soldiers' uniforms in the Afghan War are dyed khaki (the Urdu word for "dust").

1884 Sculptor Frédéric Auguste Bartholdi, aided by engineer Alexandre Gustave Eiffel, creates the Statue of Liberty, France's gift to the U.S.

1915 German meteorologist Alfred Wegener suggests that all continents were once joined together in a single landmass, "Pangaea."

1845~1945

Bigger and Better?
The Late Romantics

Wagner's musical excesses really caused an almighty uproar, as we shall see, but not everybody saw them as the beginning of the end. He had ardent supporters, notably Liszt and the songwriter and critic Hugo WOLF *(1860–1903), who thought this was the music of the future (Wagner modestly called it that, so who are we to argue?). Three young composers, looking for an alternative to the conservatism of Brahms and the lightness of the Strausses, fell under Wagner's spell: the huge orchestras and large-scale forms were soon adopted by Anton* BRUCKNER *(1824–96), Gustav* MAHLER *(1860–1911), and Richard* STRAUSS *(1864–1949).*

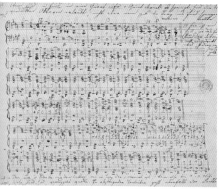

Manuscript of Bruckner's unfinished ninth symphony.

Bruckner couldn't have been less like Wagner—modest, scholarly, a devout Catholic—and wrote no operas. But when he heard Wagner's *Tannhäuser* in 1863, he realized the direction his music should take. He rejected his early, conservative style (including a "Symphony no. 0"), and launched into writing choral works and nine more symphonies, in Beethovenian mold but with Wagnerian harmonies and breadth. Sadly, they went down like a lead balloon in conservative Vienna, where he taught at the conservatory and university.

1917 Two cousins photograph fairies at Cottingley in Yorkshire; the hoax deceives Conan Doyle and others and will not be finally exposed until 1983.

1938 Superman makes his début in Action Comics; the following year the superhero will get a comic all to himself.

1955 Marian Anderson, singing the part of Ulrica in Verdi's *Masked Ball*, is the first black singer to perform at the Metropolitan Opera House in New York.

A CAST OF THOUSANDS

Mahler was a budding young composer and conductor under Bruckner in Vienna. Like his mentor, he concentrated on symphonic music rather than opera, but also wrote song cycles with orchestral accompaniment. All this was on a truly massive scale—really long, using a huge orchestra, and in several cases also solo singers and choirs (especially in symphony no. 8, the "Symphony of a Thousand"). The nine (and a bit) symphonies are all more or less autobiographical, or at least introspective, and include recurrent themes from his song cycles, culminating in a symphony masquerading as a song cycle (or vice versa): *Das Lied von der Erde* (*The Song of the Earth*).

Mahler's contemporary and lifelong friend Richard Strauss made his name writing songs and symphonic poems rather than symphonies, dealing with heroic figures rather than autobiography (although he did indulge in a bit of that in

NO, NOT THAT STRAUSS

If it sounds light, lyrical, and lilting, it's probably one of the Johanns, but if it's huge and heroically heavy, then it's Richard (no relation). And while we're on the subject, there are two Charpentiers—Marc-Antoine (Baroque stuff) and Gustave (very French, very Romantic). And whatever you do, don't confuse Weber (Romantic opera) with Webern (more on page 109).

the *Sinfonia Domestica*). But, like Mahler, he used vast orchestral resources to conjure up not only moods, but pictures in sound. Around the turn of the century, he devoted himself to operas, but returned to a more restrained classical style in his retirement, producing concertos for horn and for oboe, and the *Metamorphosen* for strings.

Jolly little devil from the cover of Strauss's *Intermezzo*.

TO WATCH

All Bruckner's symphonies deserve a hearing, but if you have to choose, go for the second, fourth, and eighth, and give the choral *Te Deum* a try too; also the sumptuously beautiful choral motets: good examples are *Os Justi* and *Locus iste*. And grab any opportunity to hear any (or better, all) of Mahler's symphonies, the song cycles *Lieder eines fahrenden Gesellen* (*Songs of a Wayfarer*), *Das Knaben Wunderhorn* (*The Boy's Magic Horn*), and *Kindertotenlieder* (*Songs on the Death of Children*), and the utterly sublime *Das Lied von der Erde*. Strauss's symphonic poems are less emotionally draining but worth looking out for (*Don Juan*, *Macbeth*, *Till Eulenspiegel*, *Don Quixote*, *Ein Heldenleben*, *Alpensinfonie*, *Sinfonia Domestica*), or if opera's your thing there's *Salome*, *Elektra*, *Der Rosenkavalier* (*The Cavalier of the Rose*), and *Die Frau ohne Schatten* (*The Woman Without a Shadow*).

WORKS

TO WATCH

WORKS

Digression

A Bunch of Keys

Before we see how it all broke down, perhaps we'd better look at the whole system of tonality—keys, chords, and scales—and the "rules," written and unwritten, that governed music from the Renaissance onward and still have their adherents today.

…Andante grazioso…

A Liszt recital: Prelude…

Let's start by sorting out what we mean by "tonality." When a piece is described as being "in the key of C," for example, that tells us that the music is based on the notes of the scale of C, and chords derived from them. Have a look at example 1a, and you'll see the scale of C major, which is simply the white notes of the piano starting on C. It goes up— tone, tone, semitone, tone, tone, tone, semitone—and back down again, and major scales in every key follow the same pattern. Minor scales follow a slightly different pattern (example 1b), but the principle is the same. The starting note of the scale is known as the tonic, and is the "tonal center" of pieces

in that key: the music tends to gravitate toward it, and the piece almost always begins and ends with it.

Make a triad on the tonic note (see example 1 again), and you've got the tonic chord, which is a bit like home base in tonal music. Triads on other notes are used to harmonize other bits of the piece, but we usually end up on the tonic chord. That's what tonality is all about— establishing a tonal center, the key of the piece, moving away from it, and returning to the "home key" again.

…Molto appassionato…

EXAMPLE 1A

Major scale   *Major triad*

EXAMPLE 1B

Minor scale   *Minor triad*

Major and minor scales starting on C, with their tonic chords. Scales in other keys follow the same patterns, starting on their tonic note.

EXAMPLE 2

Consonances   *Dissonances*

Nice (consonant) and nasty (dissonant) note combinations.

THERE AND BACK

The business of moving away from the home key, and then returning to it, creates a tension and resolution which is fundamental to tonal music. By using notes that are not part of the scale, chromatic notes, a composer can take the music into completely different keys, but still the pull of the home key is felt. Modulation (musical buzzword for changing key) is an integral part of most musical forms, from the simple binary A-B-A (home key—different key—home key) to the complex sonata form, where the composer can stray miles away from the tonic before returning home for the recapitulation.

Presto furioso...

Tension and resolution are important on a small scale too. The basic triads are built on consonances, and can be a bit bland. On the other hand, dissonances such as those in example 2 are pretty spicy, and need to be used sparingly. Dissonant chords create a tension that cries out for resolution by an appropriate consonant chord—like waiting for the other shoe to drop (example 3).

These two devices—dissonant harmony, and modulation via chromatic notes—originally evolved to emphasize the gravitational pull of the tonal center, making resolution inevitable. But they have a dramatic effect when taken out of context: dissonant and chromatic chords are often used simply for their exotic colors ("chromatic" means colored), rather than structurally. And then along came Wagner, who resolved dissonant chords onto yet more dissonances, and modulated so frequently, fluidly, and rapidly that you lose any sense of home key—and suddenly the whole system was called into question.

EXAMPLE 3

Dissonances   Resolution

Resolving a dissonant chord to a chord of C major.

...and Finale—bravo!

1893 Chicago's World's Columbian Exposition celebrates electricity; the "White City" is brilliantly lit at night and visitors can ride the first Ferris wheel.

1899 The Anglo-Boer war begins in South Africa; both sides are equipped with Vickers-Maxim weapons by Basil Zaharoff, who makes a considerable fortune.

1900 German-American composer Kurt Weill is born; his collaborations with the poet and dramatist Bertolt Brecht will be dubbed subversive and banned in Germany.

1850~1920

Some More -isms and an -ality or Two
Reaction to Romanticism

A photograph of Arnold Schoenberg, pioneer of atonality and serial composition, with a dedication to the painter Kandinsky.

In several ways, Romanticism was the architect of its own destruction. Content was increasingly taking precedence over form, and the ambiguity of the harmonic language became so intense that it began to eat away at the foundations of the tonal system. And when Wagner came on the scene and started to build his castles in the air, or at least his Schloß *on the Rhine, the whole thing began to tumble to the ground. The late nineteenth century was crisis time for Western music, and composers had to find alternatives to the crumbling edifice of tonality.*

There was another self-destruct mechanism too. Romantics had an idealized view of Nature and the peasantry, and were fascinated by mythology. In music this manifested itself in the use of folk song and folk dance, and operas and program music based on epic legends. Around the same time as Wagner's overpoweringly German operas, composers elsewhere began to ask, "Well then, what about us?", and delved into their own heritage for inspiration. The reaction to the Austrian-German monopoly of the previous century or so was a wave of nationalism—music with a refreshingly local accent.

Nationalism only partly solved the problem. The idioms may have been different, but the language was still basically the same. Some composers felt that the chromaticism of Wagner's *Tristan und Isolde* had

All That Jazz
Through the nineteenth century the U.S. was beginning to establish its own national identity, with music to match. To some extent modernism substituted for nationalism there, but at the turn of the century there came into view the germs of a specifically American, and massively influential, sound: ragtime (such as the compositions of Scott Joplin, 1868–1917) and then jazz. Beyond the scope of this little book, I'm afraid—but your cue to rush out and buy *Jazz: A Crash Course.*

1900 Italian novelist and playwright Gabriele D'Annunzio's *Il fuoco* is inspired by his long-standing affair with the actress Eleonora Duse.

1913 U.S. vaudeville performer Harry Fox executes a jerky two-step routine to ragtime music in the Ziegfeld Follies; a tamed version becomes the fox trot.

1914 The last known passenger pigeon in the U.S. dies in Cincinnati Zoo. In Wisconsin in 1871, nesting passenger pigeons had occupied 750 square miles.

sounded the death knell of tonality, and set out to find a completely new musical language. The form versus content debate became a hot issue again, and there were two very different solutions to the dilemma.

In France, the reaction was to reject the formal implications of chromatic harmony altogether and just use chords for their "color"—why choose to resolve a dissonance at all if it sounds good? The resulting expression became widely known as Impressionism (after the movement in painting doing much the same thing), creating a picture in sound.

For a while, German and Austrian composers also tried using Wagner's chromatic chords, not to depict a scene but to express their inner angst (this was, after all, the age of Freud), and there was a brief period of

FOR THOSE OF A NERVOUS DISPOSITION

We are now entering the twentieth century, and there are still people who warn you off "that modern stuff" because it's "difficult" and "tuneless." Don't listen to them—listen to the music. Don't be frightened, just relax and try to keep an open mind. It helps if you know where the composer is coming from, and what he or she is trying to achieve, but not essential. A lot of twentieth-century music is in a new musical language, and you can't expect to appreciate it at first hearing, but persevere! Familiarity often breeds insight, not contempt, and as you get to know a piece, something usually "clicks."

Expressionism. But the Viennese had a long association with classical forms and weren't too happy with all this newfound freedom; so some of them began writing a new rule book, based on the idea of a series of all 12 notes of the chromatic scale, and from this, in a triumph of form over content, Serialism was born.

Once the break with tonality had been made, composers were free to try all sorts of things: music in more than one key at once (bitonality, and even polytonality) or no key at all (atonality), dividing the scale into more than 12 notes (microtonality), harking back to the good old days (neoclassicism) . . . it was open season.

Monet's *Sunrise, Le Havre,* inspired by sea and sky. Impressionist composers were attracted to similar subjects as their contemporaries.

1855 Novelist and playwright Ivan Turgenev's play, *A Month in the Country*, is the first Russian psychological drama.

1858 A magazine editor advises a youthful correspondent "not to attempt the climbing of styles in a crinoline" and that "it would be better, in a high wind, to remain indoors."

1908 A huge fireball strikes a valley in Siberia, devastating an area the size of St. Petersburg, incinerating herds of reindeer and melting metal objects.

1850~1930
Quite a Handful
Nationalism in Russia

A eunuch from Rimsky-Korsakov's *Sheherazade*.

One of the first places nationalism showed itself was Russia. The appearance of an educated middle class produced writers such as Pushkin, Dostoevsky, and Tolstoy, and also composers searching for an indigenous style. Taking the raw materials of Russian folk music and pouring them into the mold of European classical music, they came up with a sturdy hybrid. In the mid-nineteenth century the first truly Russian operas appeared: Mikhail GLINKA's (1804–57) A Life for the Tsar *and* Ruslan and Lyudmilla, *and Alexandr DARGOMIZHSKY's (1813–69) settings of Pushkin's* Rusalka *and* The Stone Guest.

Rimsky "Improvements"

Rimsky thought he was a cut above the rest of the "Handful." He was after all a professor at the St. Petersburg Conservatory (but only one step ahead of his students). He took it upon himself to correct the "mistakes" in his colleagues' work and "improve" their orchestration—Mussorgsky suffered particularly from these attentions. But fortunately most of the (preferable) originals have survived.

With Glinka and Dargomizhsky as father figures, a group of young composers, who became known as the *moguchaya kuchka* (the "Mighty Handful"), or simply "The Five," got together around *Mily BALAKIREV* (1837–1910); the other members were *Alexander BORODIN* (1833–87), *César CUI* (1835–1918), *Modest MUSSORGSKY* (1839–81), and *Nikolay RIMSKY-KORSAKOV* (1844–1908). Their aim was simple: a nationalistic style based on Russian folk music.

GOOD ENOUGH, BORIS

Their slightly rudimentary grasp of European techniques suited the adoption of folk idioms, and gave their work a rugged originality. By the 1870s, a distinctive style had developed, and all five composed influential pieces: Borodin had completed his second symphony and much of the opera *Prince Igor*, and Mussorgsky his great opera *Boris Godunov*. But Borodin and Mussorgsky both had other jobs, composing didn't come easily to Balakirev, Cui frankly wasn't that good, and although Rimsky was technically competent and a superb orchestrator, his music is rather superficial—so masterpieces were a bit thin on the ground.

c.1916 Russian composer Alexander Glazunov, asked how many students at the conservatory are Jewish, replies, "We don't keep count."

1918 The Romanov dynasty, founded in 1613, comes to an abrupt end as Tsar Nicholas II and his family are killed at Yekaterinburg on the orders of the Bolsheviks.

1923–32 The Russian Association of Proletarian Musicians exercises a stranglehold on music composition in the Soviet Union.

Scriabin/Skryabin/Skriabin

Spell it any way you like, Alexander Skryabin (1872–1915) was odd man out among his Russian contemporaries. His interest in the mystical, especially Madam Blavatsky's theosophy, led to an idiosyncratic harmonic language. Titles like *Divine Poem, Poem of Ecstasy,* and *Prometheus: Poem of Fire* (with colored lights to match the harmonies) sum up his style.

There was, however, another Russian, the product of a conservative, sophisticated, and thoroughly European musical education: *Pyotr TCHAIKOVSKY* (1840–1893). His first symphony was just the sort of thing the "Five" were trying to get away from, but after he met Balakirev in 1867, Tchaikovsky's music took a more nationalistic turn. He was very much a loner, and felt isolated from society by his homosexuality, so he turned down Balakirev's invitation to join the "Handful," but their influence and his technical mastery combined to produce a series of very fine symphonies, one of the best known of all piano concertos, and hugely popular ballets such as *The Nutcracker* and *Swan Lake*.

After Tchaikovsky, Russian music was preoccupied with reconciling its Russianness with mainstream European trends. Two more great composers emerged, *Alexander GLAZUNOV* (1865–1936) and *Sergey RACHMANINOV* (1873–1943), but they were something of an anachronism. The twentieth century belonged to another young Russian, Stravinsky (see pages 110–11).

Rachmaninov, best known for his Romantic piano music.

TO WATCH / WORKS

Of the "Five," only three get performed much: Mussorgsky (don't miss *Boris Godunov, Night on the Bare Mountain,* and *Pictures at an Exhibition,* either the piano version or the orchestration by Ravel); Borodin (symphony no. 2, the two string quartets, and the *Polovtsian Dances* from *Prince Igor*), and Rimsky-Korsakov (*Spanish Capriccio, Sheherazade,* and the opera *The Golden Cockerel*). Tchaikovsky's symphonies are a must, especially the last three, as are the first piano concerto and *Romeo and Juliet* overture (but try the *1812* for fun). And Rachmaninov? The four piano concertos and three symphonies— real weepies.

TO WATCH / WORKS

The ballroom scene from *Swan Lake,* a perennial favorite and ideal vehicle for Tchaikovsky's passionate music.

1851 Scottish printer James Harrison notices that ether cools metal; he pumps it through pipes to cool a brewery in the gold-rush city of Bendigo, Australia.

1871 The British chancellor proposes a "match tax" of a penny per box, provoking such an outcry in Parliament and the press that the levy is abolished.

1919 Charles Fort's *Book of the Damned* chronicles unexplained phenomena and mysterious happenings in his characteristically quirky and outrageous style.

1850~1950

The Old Folk at Home
Nationalism Elsewhere

Peasant dances—inspiration to composers looking for an antidote to Wagner.

It wasn't only Russia. Just about everybody was delving into their folk heritage in the search for an alternative to Germanic Romanticism. Some émigrés, such as Chopin and Liszt, no doubt had nostalgic reasons for writing their polonaises, mazurkas, and Hungarian dances (Brahms was probably just looking for a bit of local color), but others were sick and tired of the assumption that the only good music was coming out of Germany and Austria, and to a lesser extent France and Italy. Besides, a number of countries were beginning to assert their political independence, so why should they submit to musical dictatorship?

An Australian-American Anglo-Scandinavian Nationalist
Percy Grainger (1882–1961) was born in Melbourne, studied in Frankfurt, toured Scandinavia, lived in London, and settled in the U.S. Best remembered for what he called "fripperies" (*Country Gardens, Handel in the Strand*), he was actually a serious composer whose huge output included arrangements of British and Scandinavian folk tunes, and some very experimental original works.

The Czechs were among the first to bounce in. Bohemia was still under Austrian rule, but nationalist feelings were running high; the time was ripe for *Bedřich* SMETANA (1824–84) to make his mark with a couple of operas in Czech, *The Brandenburgers in Bohemia* and *The Bartered Bride*. He went on to write several

more operas and the overtly nationalist cycle of symphonic poems *Má Vlast* (*My Country*). Following his lead, *Antonín* DVOŘÁK (1841–1904) incorporated many Czech themes and Slavonic dance rhythms into the well-established forms of the symphony and string quartet. While working in New York in 1892–95 he developed an interest in Afro-American and Native American folk music, using elements of them in the "New World" symphony, the "American" string quartet, and the cello concerto. The Czech nationalist torch was carried into the twentieth century by *Leoš* JANÁČEK

1928 The young English composer Eric Fenby becomes amanuensis to Frederick Delius, and remains so until the latter's death in 1934.

1939 After Harvard freshman Lothrop Withington Jr. swallows a live goldfish, the craze spreads to other campuses; the record is set at MIT—42 at a sitting.

(1854–1928), who used the folk music of his native Moravia to startling effect in his operas, the *Glagolitic Mass*, and the orchestral *Taras Bulba* and *Sinfonietta*.

Scandinavia was also asserting its independence from European (and Russian) domination. *Edvard GRIEG* (1843–1907), particularly in his piano miniatures and the incidental music for Ibsen's *Peer Gynt*, created a distinctly Nordic sound by using Norwegian folk themes; but the Danish *Carl NIELSEN* (1865–1931) and Finnish *Jean SIBELIUS* (1865–1957) achieved a recognizably national style in their symphonies more often by inflection than quotation or imitation of a folk style.

Sibelius's *Finlandia* and *Karelia* suite put Finland on the musical map.

The U.S.—A Special Case

A nationalist style didn't really develop in the U.S., but there were a couple of composers who drew on folk sources. Louis Moreau Gottschalk (1829–69) used Afro-American and Latin-American inflections to wonderful effect in his piano music, and Stephen Foster (1826–64) wrote several enduring minstrel songs. And the U.S. equivalent of the Strausses must be John Philip Sousa (1854–1932)—as American as apple pie.

NAMES TO NOTE

Although not overtly nationalistic, **Franz Berwald** *(1796–1868) had distinctively Swedish and* **Johan Peter Hartmann** *(1805–1900) distinctively Danish styles, and* **Edward MacDowell** *(1860–1908) was just recognizably American. On the other hand* **Enrique Granados** *(1867–1916) and* **Joaquin Rodrigo** *(b.1901) were suitably Spanish,* **Heitor Villa-Lobos** *(1887–1959) brilliantly Brazilian,* **Peter Warlock** *(1894–1930) ever so English, and* **Ignacy Paderewski** *(1860–1941) politically Polish (he became prime minister of Poland in 1919).*

Similar things were happening elsewhere. *Isaac ALBÉNIZ* (1860–1909) and *Manuel DE FALLA* (1876–1946) tapped a rich source of exciting Spanish folk music; while *Edward ELGAR* (1857–1934) and *Ethel SMYTH* (1858–1944) put an English slant on an essentially German style, laying the foundations for the unkindly nicknamed "cowpat school" led by *Ralph VAUGHAN WILLIAMS* (1872–1958) and *Gustav HOLST* (1874–1934).

Elgar's overture *Cockaigne*, a musical portrait of London.

1873 French perfume-makers at Grasse use volatile fluids to extract a solid essence from flowers and other sources of fragrance, revolutionizing the industry.

1883 Tonkin, Annam, and Cochin China become French protectorates; China refuses to recognize French control and a bloody confrontation takes place outside Hanoi.

1913 14-year-old Suzanne Lenglen becomes French tennis champion; she will win the women's singles title at Wimbledon in 1919.

1880~1940

Making a Good Impression
France

French composers didn't feel the need to dig down to their folk roots in the same way as other countries—they had a well-established musical culture going back several centuries, and had always gone their own sweet way. Even the Romantics among them had somehow retained their national identity, so when the crisis in tonality hit them, they reacted with the musical equivalent of a Gallic shrug of the shoulders and came up with something new—but with a distinctly French flavor.

Erik SATIE (1866–1925) refused to take the problem too seriously. Actually, there's little evidence he took anything very seriously. He left the Paris Conservatoire after only a year, preferring to make a meager living playing in the cafés of Montmartre. His answer to the excesses of Romanticism was understatement—where they wrote on an even bigger scale, he wrote short, simple piano pieces. And his answer to chromatic, dissonant harmony was to ignore the need for resolution—giving his music a static quality that was at odds with the drama of the Wagnerian ideal.

Debussy coaxes some new and exotic sounds from the orchestra.

Literary Connections

Although Impressionism got its name from the analogous movement in painting, it actually had more in common with the dreamy style of the Symbolist poets Charles Baudelaire, Maurice Maeterlinck, and especially Stéphane Mallarmé. Just as Goethe inspired the Romantics, Mallarmé inspired Impressionist works such as *L'Après-midi d'un faune*, and both Debussy and Ravel set his poems to music.

Claude DEBUSSY (1862–1918), however, was a diligent student at the Conservatoire under Franck and Gounod, made the pilgrimage to Wagner's Bayreuth Festivals in 1888 and 1889, and was in danger of becoming another late Romantic himself. But two things changed his mind: first, his friendship with the eccentric Satie, who showed him there was another way; and second, hearing a Javanese gamelan (percussion "orchestra").

1918 "It's raining my soul, it's raining, but it's raining dead eyes"; Italian-born French poet and critic Guillaume Apollinaire dies of a head injury sustained in 1916.

1921 Nadia Boulanger, teacher, composer, and conductor, starts teaching some of the U.S.'s best at the American Conservatory in Fontainebleau.

1941 Tinned Spam, chopped pork compressed into a loaf, becomes a staple in the diet of Allied soldiers.

'20s style par excellence: Satie and Jean Cocteau, the French poet, playwright, and film director, collaborated on the ballet *Parade*, commissioned by ballet impresario Diaghilev.

BON APRÈS-MIDI

Satiesque unresolved dissonances and restraint, combined with unconventional scales and exotic Asian timbres, produced a music where color and texture were paramount—later dubbed "Impressionism." The ethereal, floating quality of Debussy's music was a perfect antidote to all that Teutonic weight and tension, and the emphasis on sound for its own sake, not for formal or dramatic purposes, had a profound influence on twentieth-century music.

One of the first to be seduced by Impressionism was *Maurice RAVEL* (1875–1937). The idea of "color" particularly appealed to him, because he was a superbly inventive orchestrator and had an enviable ear for detail. But he took the principles of Debussy's style further by incorporating other influences into his music, including Spanish folk music, the Viennese waltz, Baroque keyboard music, and jazz.

Debussy had the technical abilities that Satie either lacked or, more likely, couldn't be bothered with, and used these seemingly disparate influences to create his own style.

And This One's Called...

Satie had a neat line in titles for his piano pieces, most of them beautifully inappropriate—for instance: *Cold pieces*, *New cold pieces*, *Dried embryos*, *Second-to-last thoughts*, *Bureaucratic Sonatina*, *Three pear-shaped pieces*, *Three flabby preludes (for a dog)*. More apt is *Vexations*, a 180-note piece to be repeated 840 times.

TO WATCH

WORKS

Satie is best known for the three *Gymnopédies* and three *Gnossiennes* for piano, but there's lots more in a similar vein, notably the *Sports et Divertissements*, and try his ballet *Parade*. Debussy wrote loads of great piano music too, such as the two sets of *Préludes*, but is at his sumptuous best in orchestral pieces—*L'Après-midi d'un faune*, *Nocturnes*, and *La Mer*—or the Maeterlinck opera *Pelléas et Mélisande*. Ravel was such a good craftsman that everything is a delight, but don't miss the two piano concertos, the string quartet, the piano pieces *Gaspard de la nuit* and *Le Tombeau de Couperin*, and the gorgeous (if hackneyed) *La Valse* and *Boléro*.

TO WATCH

WORKS

1910 German bacteriologist Paul Ehrlich produces the first synthetic drug, Salvarsan, the first effective drug treatment for syphilis.

1913 Experimenting with steel alloys, British metallurgist Harry Brearley finds a reject specimen containing 14 percent chromium, which proves rust-free.

1920 Swiss psychiatrist Hermann Rorschach devises the "inkblot test" to see into his patients' unconscious world.

1900~1945

Three in a Row...
The Second Viennese School

So, the French had found a way around the breakdown of tonality, but it wasn't a solution that suited the Germanic temperament. As we've seen, Bruckner, Mahler, and Strauss carried on almost as if nothing was wrong, but there was a composer in Vienna who recognized the implications of chromatic and dissonant harmony. Quite consciously and deliberately, he took the system to its absolute limits and beyond, and then suggested a radical but logical reorganization of the musical rule book.

Arnold Schoenberg—from chromaticism to atonality and Serialism.

SCHOENBERG (originally Schönberg) (1874–1951) started his composing career at the turn of the century, much influenced by Brahms and especially Wagner. But he soon took complexity of form and harmony to extremes. This music had no sense of home key: tonality had been replaced with atonality and he had achieved "the emancipation of dissonance." This freedom led to some pretty weird pieces exploring extremes of mood, and the style was dubbed Expressionism.

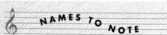
NAMES TO NOTE

Each in the next generation of composers to adopt the 12-tone system gave it a distinctive slant. **Roberto Gerhard** *(1896–1970), a Spaniard who settled in England, combined it with Spanish rhythmic and melodic inflections;* **Luigi Dallapiccola** *(1904–75) treated it with Italian lightness of touch;* **Nikos Skalkottas** *(1904–49), with Greek complexity; and* **Elizabeth Lutyens** *(1906–83) with English bloody-mindedness.*

SERIAL KILLERS

After a while, though, the freedom began to pall. Being Viennese, Schoenberg's musical ancestry was one of formal discipline, and Expressionism smacked of musical anarchy. In the 1920s he found the answer: Serialism, or 12-tone music. If, he reasoned, tonality is dead, then no one note

1920 Australian diva Nellie Melba is the first professional singer paid for a radio performance; her choice includes "Home Sweet Home."

1934 Chicago clockmaker Laurens Hammond patents the first pipeless organ; the Hammond organ is the first of a generation of electrically amplified musical instruments.

1955 Radiocarbon dating is developed by the American physicist Willard F. Libby, which means that organic remains can be accurately dated.

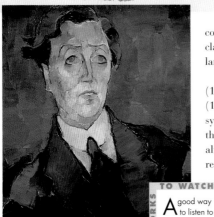

Alban Berg had a lyrical and Romantic approach to Serialism.

counterpoint, and neatly packaged in strict classical forms. A completely new musical language—wow!

Two of Schoenberg's pupils, *Alban BERG* (1885–1935) and *Anton WEBERN* (1883–1945), eagerly adopted the new system, and the three came to be known as the "Second Viennese School." Berg, although obsessed with numerology, never really gave up the tonal pull in his music, and adapted Serialism to his own lyrical style. But Webern applied 12-tone rules rigorously and uncompromisingly. His belief that each sound should stand on its own merits led to intensity and conciseness (his entire output can be heard in an afternoon), a sort of distillation of the principles of Serialism.

iis more important than the others. So, all twelve notes of the chromatic scale should be given equal importance systematically: arrange them in a series (hence "Serialism") or "tone row," and then don't repeat any note until the other 11 have sounded, in order. It's as easy as that!

Well, perhaps not that easy. Once the order of notes has been chosen, the tone row can then be turned upside down, or reversed, or subjected to all types of tricks; then it can be used as a basis for harmony and

WORKS TO WATCH

A good way to listen to Schoenberg is chronologically, starting with the Romantic *Gurrelieder* and *Verklärte Nacht*, and the chamber symphony no.1, then the Expressionist *Five Orchestral Pieces*, *Erwartung*, and *Pierrot Lunaire*, before tackling the 12-tone suite op. 25 for piano, third string quartet, and variations for orchestra, then the unfinished opera *Moses und Aaron*, and *A Survivor from Warsaw*. Berg is more approachable—try the *Lyric Suite*, the violin concerto, and the operas *Wozzeck* and *Lulu*—but Webern does take some getting used to. Look out for the *Six Pieces for Orchestra*, and six songs op.14.

Serial Destinies

Schoenberg, a Jew, fled to the U.S. in the 1930s. Webern wasn't Jewish, but because of his associates (and his music), he suffered personally, professionally, and financially under the regime of the Third Reich. In a cruel twist of fate, he was accidentally shot dead by an American soldier just after liberation. Berg didn't do much better; he was spared the atrocities of the Nazis, but only because he died of blood poisoning as the result of an insect bite.

1914 The first traffic lights are introduced in Cleveland, Ohio.

1918 Ernest Ansermet founds the Orchestre de la Suisse Romande; he has conducted Diaghilev's Ballets Russes since 1915, and premiered many of Stravinsky's works.

1929 Josef Stalin exiles Leon Trotsky and 1600 of his followers to Siberia for "anti-Soviet" activities; Trotsky has already been expelled from the party.

1882~1971

...And One of a Kind
Stravinsky

While Debussy and Schoenberg were dealing with the chaos that Wagner had left behind, young Igor STRAVINSKY (1882–1971) was learning his craft with Rimsky-Korsakov, and composing his first pieces in the Russian nationalist style. It was good stuff, too, getting him a commission to write music for the Ballets Russes, but didn't give any indication that he was going to become one of the most original composers of the twentieth century, bursting onto the European scene with a violently avant-garde ballet score that turned Western musical thinking on its head.

A figure from *The Firebird*, Stravinsky's first Ballets Russes hit.

Russian ballet was popular at the time and Stravinsky had his first big success in 1910 with *The Firebird*, which the Ballets Russes took to Paris. On the strength of this he was commissioned to write more for the company. What he came up with was *Petrouchka*, an innocent enough story, the Russian equivalent of *Punch and Judy*. But the music was something else—sure, it was based on folk tunes, but traditional form was all but abandoned, replaced by great "blocks" of music, sometimes in two keys at the same time (bitonal).

THAT'S RITE!

Petrouchka was a bit of a shock, but his next ballet, *Le Sacre du printemps* (*The Rite of Spring*), provoked a riot. Literally. Nobody was ready for this extraordinary portrayal of ancient fertility rites,

The stage curtain for *Petrouchka*. Stravinsky's music baffled the audience.

1956 The first Eurovision Song Contest is held in Lugano; the winner is the Swiss Lyss Alyssia.

1962 Stravinsky visits Leningrad and Moscow and is received by Nikita Khrushchev—after decades of sanctioned attacks he can now be "rehabilitated."

1968 A laboratory in St. Paul, Minnesota, researching superglue, discovers an adhesive that comes unstuck; in 1980, 3M sells the first Post-it Notes.

Sergey Diaghilev, the impresario behind Stravinsky's early successes in Paris.

with savage harmonies and irregularly pounding rhythms. Primitive, ritualistic, breathtakingly modern, and the single most influential piece of twentieth-century music. Wow.

Stravinsky quieted down a bit after the *Rite*, writing smaller-scale pieces on Russian folk themes, such as *Les Noces* and *The Soldier's Tale*. Then, in the 1920s, he changed tack again with another ballet, *Pulcinella*, based on themes attributed to the eighteenth-century composer Pergolesi. This marked the beginning of a period of Neoclassicism, reworking Baroque and classical forms and styles in his own inimitable way.

Rhythmic drive and dry textures (incorporating some elements of jazz) are typical of his 1920s and '30s music, which includes the

opera/oratorio *Oedipus Rex* and the Bach-like *Dumbarton Oaks* concerto. He never quite gave up his Russian roots, though, arranging pieces by Tchaikovsky for the ballet *Le Baiser de la fée*, and, after rejoining the Orthodox Church, composing the *Symphony of Psalms*.

In 1939 he moved to the U.S., where he wrote the last of his Neoclassical pieces and then started to take an interest in serial music. He was working on the ballet *Agon* at the time, and during its composition developed his own serial style (you can actually hear it emerge during the course of the piece—fascinating). Stravinsky's 12-tone period was devoted to religious works in a rather stark, austere style, such as *Requiem Canticles*, which was performed at his funeral in Venice.

Shall We Dance?

Stravinsky's early successes were with ballets commissioned by Sergey Diaghilev for his Ballets Russes, who were the darlings of the Paris scene—especially with Vaslav Nijinsky as leading man. The collaboration continued until Diaghilev's death in 1929, when Stravinsky teamed up with George Balanchine, a Russian defector to the West, in an equally fruitful partnership.

What a Performance

The *Rite of Spring* was premiered in Paris in 1913. Half the audience was carried away by the music, but the other half felt they were being taken for a ride. Feelings ran high; the listeners divided into opposing factions and fistfights broke out, but the band played on. Difficult to imagine any other piece having quite the same effect...

1908 After successfully splitting the world's largest diamond, the Cullinan, master gem cutter Joseph Asscher faints with relief.

1921 Karel Capek coins the word "robot" (in Czech, *robota* means "slave") in his prophetic play *Rossum's Universal Robot*.

1952 Marine archaeologist Jacques Cousteau discovers an ancient Greek ship off the coast of Marseilles; its cargo—3,000 wine urns—survives.

1900~1967

Collectors' Items

Hungary

Nationalism didn't really get going in Hungary as quickly as elsewhere—unless you count Brahms and Liszt and their Hungarian dances and rhapsodies. The Habsburg Empire ruled over the territory until 1918, and Viennese influence was strong, but many Hungarians had a powerful sense of national identity. A couple of young composers met up in Budapest just after the turn of the century, and discovered they both wanted to write in a truly Hungarian style, incorporating native folk song into their music. So, Béla BARTÓK (1881–1945) and Zoltán KODÁLY (1882–1967) set off together to collect folk songs systematically, using the latest recording techniques.

Zoltán Kodály, who collected folk music with Bartók.

Bartók's piano pieces *For Children* are based on Slovakian folk tunes.

What they found was a source of material richer than they had hoped for: not the gypsy violin music of the city cafés, but real Magyar peasant music, and lots of it. At first they restricted themselves to Hungary, but their later field trips extended into neighboring Romania, Transylvania, and Slovakia. The traveling came to an end with the First World War, but they had already built up an impressive catalogue and established themselves among the first ethnomusicologists (great word meaning people who study music of various cultures).

Other Folk

There was a craze for collecting folk music in the late nineteenth and early twentieth centuries. In Britain the Reverend Sabine Baring-Gould, Cecil Sharp, Ralph Vaughan Williams, Percy Grainger, A.L. Lloyd, and Ewan MacColl all made significant contributions, some using their findings in their own music. Sharp also collected in North America (especially the Appalachians), followed by John Jacob Niles, Alan Lomax, Charles Seeger, and the whole American "Folk Revival" of the 1950s.

1956 The Hungarian uprising is brutally crushed by the Red Army; appeals to the West fall on deaf ears.

1959 Christopher Cockerell's hovercraft is the first to cross the English Channel, 50 years after Louis Blériot's first cross-Channel airplane flight.

1961 The 16-volume *Deutsches Wörterbuch*, begun in 1838 by the Brothers Grimm, covering the German language from the fifteenth century, is finally completed.

Folk Meets Modernism

The dilemma facing composers at this time was: either come up with something totally new, like Schoenberg, or go the Neoclassical or nationalist way and look to your roots for inspiration. Bartók managed to do both. The folk element is there, but only in essence, and used as the basis for completely original and modern music.

Bartók and Kodály also took an interest in what was happening in the contemporary classical scene, studying composers as diverse as Richard Strauss and Debussy, and integrating elements of these artists' styles into their own music. By 1910, when their first string quartets were premiered, they had developed a distinctive modern Hungarian sound.

Kodály restricted himself to Magyar folk music, using tunes he had collected as themes in his work, and established himself as a truly Hungarian composer at around the time Hungary gained its independence. Bartók, however, spread his

net wider and took the process further. He drew on sources from all over Eastern Europe, and even Turkey and North Africa, and his research into folk music whetted his appetite for exotic scales and modes. Not content with merely quoting or imitating, he tried to capture the essence of his findings by detailed analysis and reconstruction, adding his own personal slant. He was not only meticulous in his work, but also reserved and introverted (a quality that was refreshingly unlike his contemporary Stravinsky), and this shows in his music. Okay, he could, when he wanted, write exuberant dance-inspired music for orchestra, and his three stage works are at times violently expressive, but even when writing on a large scale he tends to be rather broodingly introspective. He was more comfortable with piano and chamber music, where, especially in the six string quartets, he emerged as one of the giants of music in the twentieth century.

Judith finds out more than she bargained for in Bartók's *Duke Bluebeard's Castle*.

TO WATCH

WORKS

You'll enjoy Kodály. Everybody does. Especially the orchestral music—the suite from his opera *Háry János* is fun, and so are the *Dances of Galánta*, *Dances of Marosszék*, and the *Peacock Variations*. For the more serious side, try the two string quartets or the glorious *Psalmus Hungaricus*. Bartók's last work, the *Concerto for Orchestra*, is perhaps the most approachable, but give the *Music for Strings, Percussion and Celesta* a try too. And there's always the opera *Duke Bluebeard's Castle*, the ballet *The Wooden Prince*, or the mime drama *The Miraculous Mandarin*. But the best stuff, in my opinion, is in the six string quartets, the three piano concertos, and the amazing *Sonata for Two Pianos and Percussion*.

1925 French actress and writer Colette's scenario for a fantasy ballet *L'Enfant et les sortilèges*, is turned into an opera by Maurice Ravel.

1928 French musician Maurice Martenot invents the Ondes musicales, a radio-electric instrument later known as Ondes Martenot.

1940 Saved from a death from rabies in 1885 by Louis Pasteur, Joseph Meister kills himself rather than open Pasteur's tomb for the Nazis.

1920~1980

The French Connection II

Les Six

WORKS

TO WATCH

Poulenc's *Les Biches, Concert champêtre*, and concerto for organ are played quite often, but look out for the *Stabat Mater* and the *Gloria* too. Milhaud wrote massive amounts; you're likely to come across *Le Boeuf sur le toit* and the *Suite provençale*. Try Honegger's *Pacific 231* (descriptive of a train), *Rugby* (the contact sport), and the nameless no. 3. Oh yes, there's Gershwin too: pop classics—*An American in Paris, Rhapsody in Blue*, the piano concerto in F, *Porgy and Bess*, songs like "Summertime," "I Got Rhythm" ...who could ask for anything more?

TO WATCH

WORKS

Debussy may have created a very French alternative to Romanticism, and had a profound influence on many composers, but it didn't suit everybody. Not even, it would appear, the next generation of French composers. In 1917, just before Debussy died, a group calling themselves Les Six—*Francis* POULENC *(1899–1963), Darius* MILHAUD *(1892–1974), Arthur* HONEGGER *(1892–1955), Georges* AURIC *(1899–1983), Louis* DUREY *(1888–1979), and Germaine* TAILLEFERRE *(1892–1983)—got together with a manifesto which rejected not only Germanic Romanticism and Russian nationalism, but also home-grown Impressionism. They were quite friendly with Jean Cocteau, who influenced their choice of literature, vaudeville, and circus as inspiration.*

T he result was witty, charming, and unsentimental music which owed a lot to Satie's understated piano style

Milhaud, Cocteau, and Poulenc, with unknown smiling gate crasher.

and the popular music played in Parisian cafés. Also, they learned a trick or two from Stravinsky— bitonality and neoclassicism, for example. The Six went their separate ways in the mid-1920s, but had already made quite an impact on French music.

1943 Over a million people die of starvation in Bengal.

1947 Christian Dior's "New Look" collection is launched in Paris; the British government condemns it as "irresponsibly frivolous."

1952 British architect Michael Ventris, analyzing Cretan inscribed clay tablets, breaks the code and deciphers Linear B script.

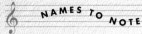

NAMES TO NOTE

There were, of course, others who were not members of Les Six. *One who might have been, had she not died so young, was* **Lili Boulanger** *(1893–1918), sister of Nadia.* **Jacques Ibert** *(1890–1962) was another who wrote in a similar vein (don't miss his* Divertissement*), and their natural successors in the next generation include* **Jean Francaix** *(b.1912) and* **Henri Dutilleux** *(b.1916).*

Les Six pose around a pretty young thing, ignoring the conductor in the background.

An American in Paris

Paris was very trendy in the interwar years. Stravinsky made it his home, and composers from the U.S. rushed over to study the Neoclassical style with his protégée Nadia Boulanger. American jazz thrived there too, influencing a whole generation of classical composers. So let's not forget Gershwin (1898–1937), who gave classical music the jazz treatment (or vice versa). Not generally considered a "classical" composer, but why not?

More enduring favorites of the group are Milhaud and Poulenc. Milhaud was posted to Brazil during the First World War, and there is a jazzy South American flavor to much of his work. Poulenc seems more urbane and worldly, verging on the superficial, but in fact beneath the veneer of pastiche and flippancy often lurked a quite serious and sincere musician. Perhaps because of their perceived "facile" approach, *Les Six* didn't establish a particular following, but there was a young composer around who did—Olivier Messiaen. More later on pages 124–25.

Honegger was the odd man out in more ways than one: although born in France, he was Swiss; and he had a tendency toward (gasp!) Romanticism. He made his name with an oratorio, *Le Roi David*, but his orchestral music, especially the five symphonies, shows him at his very best. If he was the odd man out, then Tailleferre was the odd woman—she was a brilliantly talented composer by all accounts, but is almost never heard today for some reason. Is she, like Auric and Durey, simply out of fashion, or might it have something to do with her gender?

1900 To photograph its luxury train, the Chicago Railroad Company employs a 12-foot-long camera; each photo is the size of a door.

1919 Augustus D. Juilliard's bequest enables the Juilliard School of Music to be founded in New York City.

1922 A dog, accidentally left behind when his master's ship left Vancouver for Yokohama, finds his own way to Japan and is reunited with his owner.

1900~1950

The Wild West

United States

It took a long time for the U.S. to assert its musical independence. Until about 1900, musicians seemed to cling fiercely to their roots—white composers followed European trends (with pretty pale imitations, most of the time); and although black musicians had developed a strong folk style, its acceptance by the mainstream was as slow in coming as their real emancipation. The turn of the century brought two remarkable changes. For black music it was ragtime, and the emergence of jazz. For lily-white, conservative America it was an iconoclast called Charles IVES (1874–1954).

Charles Ives: a sophisticated blend of Americana and modernity.

On the face of it, Ives was nothing out of the ordinary: he was the son of a bandmaster in small-town New England, studied music at Yale, and had a successful career in insurance. But his music is uncompromisingly experimental, using dissonant, atonal harmonies and complex rhythms, often achieved by playing in not only different keys but also different tempos simultaneously, and even using microtones and deliberate "wrong notes." The sound of two amateur bands marching past each other left a strong childhood impression on Ives.

PIONEERS

Ives lived in New York for much of his life, becoming a close friend of another New Englander, *Carl RUGGLES* (1876–1971). Like Ives, he associated himself with the rugged Transcendentalist philosophy of Thoreau and Emerson, and composed in a suitably vigorous chromatic style—but,

Play It Again, Sam

Cowell dropped into his local music store to hear a piano roll of one of his compositions. When the assistant put it into a Pianola, whole sections of the keyboard went down and crashing noises came out of the machine—just what Cowell had written. The assistant apologized to the mischievous composer for the dud roll, and fetched another, then another . . .

1950 American businessman Frank McNamara introduces the Diners Club charge card—and ushers in the credit card revolution.

1955 Blue jeans, once hard-wearing workwear, become fashionable for the young.

1956 Elvis Presley, whose music was influenced by folk tradition, has a string of pop hits. A fan describes him as "...just one big hunk of forbidden fruit."

NAMES TO NOTE

Other Americans worth looking out for include Romantic/Impressionist **Charles T. Griffes** *(1884–1920), noisy "Bad Boy of Music"* **George Antheil** *(1900–59), cooly unsentimental* **Virgil Thomson** *(1896–1989), experimentally folky* **Ruth Crawford Seeger** *(1901–53), conservative* **Samuel Barber** *(1910–81) (composer of the enormously successful* Adagio *for strings), popular and jazz-inspired* **Leonard Bernstein** *(1918–90), and Serialist* **Milton Babbitt** *(b.1916).*

like Webern, distilling it into a total output of about three hours of music. Also working in New York was *Edgard Varèse* (1883–1965), a Frenchman who composed in blocks of rhythmic, percussive, and extremely dissonant sound, and was one of the first of the modern generation to use electronic instruments. Meanwhile, on the West Coast, *Henry Cowell* (1897–1965) was taking a similarly radical approach, experimenting with complex polyrhythms and new techniques for playing the piano—plucking and scraping the strings inside, and playing "clusters" of notes on the keyboard with the fist or forearm.

SETTLERS

The first generation of truly American composers set a revolutionary precedent, and it was a hard act to follow. Some, such as *Aaron Copland* (1900–1990), tempered their experimentalism with the Neoclassicism they had learned from Stravinsky and Nadia Boulanger, and with elements of jazz, folk, and popular music to create a more approachable American idiom. Others, in particular *Elliott Carter* (b.1908), chose to go even further down the road of complexity, modernity, and experiment, which had become as much the language of American classical music as jazz had for black composers.

WORKS TO WATCH

Ives is his most "Ivesian" in orchestral music such as *Three Places in New England*, *Central Park in the Dark*, and *The Unanswered Question*. Chances to hear Ruggles are depressingly few, although you might catch *Men and Mountains* or *Suntreader*; Cowell is almost as rare, but keep your eyes open for his piano pieces. Varèse gets a better airing these days: don't miss *Amériques* and *Déserts* for electronic sounds and orchestra. Most of us know Copland's *Fanfare for the Common Man*, *Appalachian Spring*, and *Rodeo*, but try his more experimental piano variations.

West Side Story—Bernstein gives *Romeo and Juliet* the New York treatment.

1919 German revolutionaries Rosa Luxemburg and Karl Liebknecht are murdered by soldiers after attempting to stage a Communist coup in Berlin.

1925 A Red Army general pursuing White Army forces in southern Russia finds a wild, hairy, manlike creature—or a relic of an even earlier man?

1936 Stalin, outraged by Shostakovich's *Lady Macbeth of Mtsensk*, dictates the editorial "Muddle Instead of Music" in *Pravda*, unleashing a vicious campaign.

1920 to the present

Comrades

Behind the Iron Curtain

Music for workers on the factory floor.

The Revolution came as a bit of a blow to Russian nationalist music. Okay, it used good solid peasant tunes, but its tone was often middle-class intellectual, or suspiciously tsarist. That was all right for pre-Soviet composers, they didn't know any better, but composers under the new regime had to toe the Party line. Stalin was extremely picky about this, and made life very uncomfortable for those whose music was bourgeois or "formalistic" (a catch-all term meaning, I think, too modern for Uncle Joe to understand). This posed a problem for Soviet composers wanting to write exciting new music.

The simple answer was to produce worthy and inspiring scores for the workers, extolling the virtues of the system—which many did, but it wasn't exactly riveting stuff (although maybe riveters enjoyed it). Another option was to carry on in a nationalist style, like the

Sorry?

After being raked over the coals for "petty-bourgeois sensationalism" in the fourth symphony, Shostakovich produced a fifth symphony, seen as "a Soviet artist's practical creative reply to just criticism" by the Party. Hmm . . . listen a bit more carefully, comrades, and you'll detect in it a hefty dose of sarcasm, especially in the hollow pomposity of the last movement. In a broad sense much of Shostakovich's music was an "artist's creative reply" to intense pressures from both within and without.

Despite Party disapproval, Shostakovich was the leading Soviet composer during the Communist era. For much of his life he trod a difficult tightrope.

...and the Bamboo Curtain

Music in China has been under state control since Confucius, preserving a Chinese classical tradition going back thousands of years. After the Cultural Revolution, however, new music was restricted to pieces in a nonelitist (simplistic) blend of Western classical and clichéd Chinese styles praising Maoist socialism. A particularly good (or bad) example is the excruciating *Yellow River Concerto*, written by a committee.

1949 The world's first disposable diapers are marketed by Robinson's of Chesterfield, a British firm.

1959 More than two million East Germans have crossed over to West Germany since 1945.

1986 When the nuclear reactor at Chernobyl catches fire, it takes more than two weeks before the fire is extinguished and the release of radiation is stopped.

Armenian *Aram KHACHATURIAN* (1903–78) did, but substituting folk with Soviet heroes.

Or you could just leave the country. *Sergey PROKOFIEV* (1891–1953), already famous as an ultramodernist (and a superb craftsman), left Russia in 1918 as the Soviet Union was being formed. He settled in Paris, but wasn't really happy away from home; after several visits back to Russia he returned permanently in 1933. This involved an uneasy compromise—he had to simplify his music to please Stalin. Even so, he didn't escape criticism, and several pieces didn't get repeat performances until after he died—the same day as Stalin.

Dmitry SHOSTAKOVICH (1906–75) stayed in Russia, and had to find ways around the system. He got away with it most of the time by ostensibly adopting a style of "socialist realism," but a lot of the time sardonically parodying the establishment,

tongue firmly in cheek. Or foot in mouth, in the opera *Lady Macbeth of Mtsensk*, his first major clash with Stalin, and on several subsequent occasions. Even after Stalin died, he found it difficult to reconcile his music with the system, and there is a streak of bitter irony running through all his work.

POST-SOVIET MUSIC

Since the Iron Curtain lifted, several composers who were struggling under the system have surfaced. *Alfred SCHNITTKE* (1934–98) experimented with avant-garde techniques such as Serialism, "textural" music (more about that on page 128), but post-USSR developed his own "'polystylism," with much quotation and allusion. *Arvo PÄRT* (b.1935), an Estonian, also started out as a serial composer, but since independence has become more conservative, influenced by medieval music.

TO WATCH

WORKS

Khachaturian's ballets *Gayane* (including the famous "Saber Dance") and *Spartacus* have been consistently popular, but look out for his piano concerto too. For "pre-Soviet" Prokofiev, there's the first piano concerto, first violin concerto, symphonies nos.1 (the "Classical") and 3. After his return to the USSR there's *Romeo and Juliet, Peter and the Wolf*, and *Lieutenant Kije* and *Alexander Nevsky*, but perhaps the best work of this period is the symphony no. 5. Shostakovich's opera *Lady Macbeth of Mtsensk* is really worth seeing, but more typical are the 15 string quartets, concertos (two each for piano, cello, violin), and symphonies (1, 5, 7, 10, 14, and 15 are particularly good).

TO WATCH

WORKS

1936 Railroad construction workers in Baghdad discover an ancient grave containing a primitive electric battery, pre-dating Galvani by 15,000 years.

1939 Police in Indianapolis introduce Dr. Rolla N. Harger's "Drunkometer"—the first Breathalyzer.

1944 "D-Day"; under the supreme command of General Eisenhower, 176,000 Allied troops land at Normandy beaches.

1900 to the present

Loose Ends
A Few More Odds and Ends

Twentieth-century pick and mix.

There are quite a few composers who don't fit neatly into the main movements or national styles of twentieth-century music—some, such as Stravinsky, we've dealt with already. But there are others, especially the many Germans who didn't take up Serialism, and the English composers who broke away from the "cowpat" image, who all made their mark one way or another. A mixed bag, then, of fairly eclectic composers, just off the mainstream, but no less important for that.

L et's start with *Ferruccio BUSONI* (1866–1924), a German-Italian who tried to reconcile the conflict of German seriousness and Italian lyricism, and also the influences of classicism, Romanticism, and modernism. Most of the time, unfortunately, he didn't really succeed, but his work (and the prescient *Sketch of a New Aesthetic of Music*) was influential.

DEGENERATES

One of Busoni's pupils was *Kurt WEILL* (1900–50), who developed a blend of Romantic and popular song for his collaboration with Bertolt Brecht. His sharp, jagged music underlined the

Music on the Big Screen

The cinema has provided many composers with inspiration (and a useful source of income). Prokofiev, Shostakovich, Hindemith, Britten, Walton, Lutyens, Copland, Bernstein, and Nyman have all written film scores, and several composers do almost nothing else—Miklos Rosza, Erich Korngold, Dimitri Tiomkin, Bernard Herrmann, and John Williams, for example. Hollywood has also hijacked existing music for its own ends (particularly in *Fantasia* and *2001: A Space Odyssey*, and the ubiquitous Barber *Adagio*), but I suppose it has introduced pieces to a new audience.

Socialist Weill's music bombed in Nazi Germany.

political bite of Brecht's texts, and earned him the title "degenerate" by the Nazis (being Jewish didn't help). Weill's colleague *Paul HINDEMITH* (1895–1963), another "degenerate," was not as overtly political, but deliberately avoided the esoteric and avant-garde in what became known as *Gebrauchmusik* (music for use)—music for ordinary people to listen to and to play.

1955 Luciano Berio and Bruno Maderna found an electronic *Studio di Fonologia* at the Italian radio station in Milan.

1956 Swiss engineer Georges de Metral observes the way burrs stick to socks and invents Velcro, the peelable fastening.

1956 For *The Man with the Golden Arm*, Saul Bass designs an animated sequence for the credits, revolutionizing filmmakers' approach to titles.

and for use in the cinema, radio, and education. Music education was important in the work of *Carl Orff* (1895–1982), who composed in an accessible style influenced by Stravinsky, notably in *Carmina Burana*. *Hans Werner Henze* (b.1926), like Weill, uses his music as a vehicle for his socialist convictions, and often in a bewildering variety of styles, from neoclassicism to Serialism and jazz.

PASTURES NEW

A number of composers, just because they're English, have been inaccurately classified as an English "school." In the case of *Frederick Delius* (1862–1934) it's very strange. Although he was born in England, his family was German, he studied in Florida and Germany, and lived much of his life in France. And it shows in his music, even though he did write a few English "pastoral" pieces.

Futurists

The aim of Futurism, mainly a visual-arts movement, was to create an art appropriate to the machine age. The idea was taken up by the composer Francesco Pratella (1880–1955) and the painter-turned-composer Luigi Russolo (1885–1947), who invented new instruments, *intonarumori* (noise intoners), for their new music. Unfortunately their enthusiasm wasn't matched by their talent, and little of their music (and none of the instruments) has survived.

William Walton (1902–83) was similarly cosmopolitan, showing influences of Schoenberg, Stravinsky, and *Les Six*. But two composers dominate the postwar English scene: *Benjamin Britten* (1913–76) and *Michael Tippett* (1905–98). Both formed their own distinctive styles—Britten in an acerbic but accessible tonal style, and Tippett by absorbing exotic, avant-garde, and popular influences— a true eclectic.

Hans Werner Henze waxes lyrical conducting his own work.

TO WATCH

WORKS

Hindemith wrote loads, but the key works to look out for are the opera *Mathis der Maler* and the symphony of the same name, and the series of pieces called *Kammermusik*. The best of Weill's music is in the operettas he wrote with Brecht, *Mahagonny* and *Der Dreigroschenoper*. Henze is best known for his operas, but there's also the ballet *Orpheus*, plus symphonies, piano concertos, and string quartets to choose from. Likewise, Britten and Tippett are primarily opera composers, but listen for Britten's arrangements of folk songs, the *Young Person's Guide to the Orchestra* (not just for young persons), and the magnificent *War Requiem*; and Tippett's *Fantasia Concertante on a Theme by Corelli*, four symphonies, five string quartets, and the oratorios *A Child of Our Time* and *The Mask of Time*.

WORKS

TO WATCH

Digression

Electrifying!

Innovations in technology have often inspired composers to explore their musical possibilities and develop new styles; conversely, the demands of composers often prompted the invention of new or improved instruments—the change from viols to violins as Renaissance moved into Baroque, harpsichord to piano in the eighteenth century, and improvements in woodwind and brass instruments as the orchestra grew, were all both cause and effect. Perhaps not entirely coincidentally, as classical music underwent yet another radical change at the turn of the century, sound recording, broadcasting, and electronic instruments were being developed.

Sound recording had the same revolutionary impact as music printing had done 400 years earlier. Here was a means of recording not only the notes but actual performances, and making them accessible to a whole new audience. It was a useful tool for musicians too: performers could listen to themselves critically, folk and jazz could be recorded for posterity, and composers could play around with prerecorded sound (especially after the invention of magnetic tape). Come the 1920s, the

Digital recording and CDs have given us near-perfect reproduction.

audience was widened even further by radio; and now, with stereo broadcasts and digital recording on CD, it's almost as good as hearing live music. More people than ever before are listening to professional performances in their own homes—although whether this has been good or bad for classical music is still hotly debated.

At the same time, electronic musical instruments started to appear. As early as the 1890s there were experimental instruments such as the Telharmonium, followed in the 1920s by the Russian Theremin and French Ondes

From wax cylinders to LPs, the gramophone reigned for almost 100 years.

Martenot, but few composers showed any interest in the new instruments until after the Second World War (it took about a hundred years for the piano to really catch on, so this was quite speedy progress). At first they were seen as additions to the traditional ensembles, or (as in the case of the Hammond organ) substitutes for acoustic instruments, but technology was advancing so rapidly that a completely new form of music had to evolve to exploit its capabilities.

There were two schools of thought as to how electronic music should be composed. In the RTF studios in Paris, Pierre Schaeffer and Pierre Henri were experimenting with magnetic tape, recording all sorts of sounds (musical and nonmusical), then manipulating them in various ways— playing them at different speeds, or backward, and cutting and editing the tapes—to make what they called *musique concrète*. Meanwhile, at the WDR studios in Cologne, Werner Meyer Eppler and Herbert Eimer manipulated electronically produced sounds from oscillators by means of electronic filters and modulators to make "pure" electronic music. After some initial rivalry, the two methods were integrated

Magnetic tape played a pivotal role in the growth of electronic music.

in a form of music using a variety of sound sources by such composers as Stockhausen and Berio.

In these early days, electronic music was restricted to the studios and recorded onto tape for subsequent performance, sometimes in conjunction with traditional instruments. But as the new instruments became more portable, particularly with the advent of the digital synthesizer, they could be used live, and computer technology meant that live synthesis and manipulation of sound could be achieved in the concert hall. Electronic studios all over the world, notably at Stanford and Princeton Universities in the U.S., and IRCAM in Paris under the direction of Pierre Boulez, are now exploring the possibilities of electronic technology. The music of the future? Perhaps...

Electric guitars: ubiquitous in pop, but not very much used by "serious" composers.

1950 Immanuel Velikovsky suggests that random, rare, violent events have shaped our evolution —the theory of catastrophism.

1953 L. Ron Hubbard founds the Scientology movement in the U.S. Members use Dianetics, a method of psychotherapy, to achieve better mental health.

1956 Professor W. A. Lewis calculates that if the world population doubles every 25 years, by 2330 "there would be standing room only."

1945 to the present
The End of Time, and After
Messiaen and His Pupils

Olivier MESSIAEN (1908–92) is almost impossible to pigeonhole. His music is strikingly original, bewilderingly eclectic, not falling into any -ism or -ality, and is pretty well inimitable, so he hasn't founded any particular "school" of composition. Nevertheless, his influence has been enormous, particularly among his pupils at the Paris Conservatoire in the 1940s and '50s, who included some of the most radical composers of the century. And he wasn't above picking up a few ideas from them too.

NAMES TO NOTE

*In Italy, **Luigi Nono** (1924–90) carried on in the serial tradition (he married one of Schoenberg's daughters), and **Luciano Berio** (b.1925), associated with Boulez and Stockhausen in the '50s, developed a very personal style linked to literature, drama, and linguistics. The British composers **Harrison Birtwistle** (b.1934), **Peter Maxwell Davies** (b.1934), and **Alexander Goehr** (b.1932), contemporaries at the Royal Manchester College of Music in the 1950s, were also influenced by Messiaen, Stockhausen, and Boulez.*

For the Birds

Two themes run through much of Messiaen's music: Catholicism and birdsong. Although the former is a recurrent inspiration in music, no other composer has used the latter so consistently and thoroughly. Works such as *Réveil des oiseaux*, *Oiseaux exotiques*, and the huge *Catalogue des oiseaux* are based on his own transcriptions of birdsong collected over a lifetime, and his only opera is (what else?) *St. François d'Assise*.

Like Debussy, Messiaen had a keen ear for harmony and instrumentation, and was fascinated by modes and scales. He developed a system of modes of his own invention, and of rhythmic "modes" influenced by Indian music and Greek poetry, which form the basis of works such as the *Quatuor pour la fin du temps*, written for himself and three fellow prisoners in a German Stalag, and the sensuous *Turangalîla-symphonie*.

1962 Texan troubleshooter Red Adair extinguishes a 30-foot-high oil-well fire in the Sahara by detonating a huge explosion to blow out the fire.

1966 For the movie *One Million Years B.C.*, British special-effects man Les Bowie creates the world in six days, using porridge for lava; his fee is £2,500.

1989 The world has more than 555 million motor vehicles in use, with about 28 million being added each year.

LET'S GET ORGANIZED

Some of his pupils, however, were more interested in the serial techniques of Schoenberg and especially Webern. Messiaen encouraged their experiments with Serialism, and some of it rubbed off on him. His *Quatre études de rhythme* for piano and the *Livre d'orgue* show a systematic organization not only of pitch but also duration and intensity of notes—his own version of the total Serialism his students were trying to achieve.

So, who were these students? Well, among many others, there were Iannis Xenakis (more on him later), *Pierre Boulez* (b.1925), and *Karlheinz Stockhausen* (b.1928). Boulez had already studied mathematics, so total Serialism really appealed, and led to pieces such as the *Livre pour quatuor* (later revised as *Livre pour cordes*—he's constantly revising all his work) and *Structures*. He also has his teacher's love of the exotic and colorful, evident in *Le Marteau sans maître* and also in his orchestral and electronic pieces.

Stockhausen was one of the pioneers of electronic music in the Cologne studio,

Performances of Stockhausen's music are often theatrical affairs.

Light Music

Since about 1977, Stockhausen has devoted most of his time to a cycle of seven operas, known collectively as *Licht*, designed to be performed on seven consecutive nights. Four have so far been completed, imaginatively titled *Donnerstag*, *Samstag*, *Montag*, and *Dienstag*. Because Stockhausen is not known for his modesty, and members of his family have been involved in performances of the cycle, comparisons with Wagner's *Ring* are inevitable.

Karlheinz Stockhausen, one of the first great electronic composers, and self-confessed genius of postwar music.

producing the first masterpieces in the genre, such as *Gesang der Jünglinge* and *Kontakte*. At the same time, he was working toward a system of total Serialism where each note is meticulously accounted for, culminating in the mighty *Gruppen* for three orchestras. He then moved toward the use of live electronic manipulation of instrumental music, and chance procedures. In this he was influenced by John Cage (we'll come to him on the following page), eventually giving up notation altogether in *Aus den Sieben Tagen*, a set of prose poems, which merely suggest performance. Later works have returned to more conventional notation and development of melodic themes.

1945 Arnold Schoenberg's application for a Guggenheim Fellowship to finish an opera, an oratorio, and three works in progress is rejected.

1953 *Kismet*, a musical based on Alexander Borodin's music for *Prince Igor*, is produced in the U.S.

1957 Excavations to the foundations of New York's Harlem Hospital release an inexplicable gush of pure, warm water, flowing at 1,760 gallons per minute.

1945~1992

Anything Goes ...
Noise, Chance, and Silence

Most of the pioneers of American music were based in and around New York, and most were New Englanders. The exception, and in some ways the most iconoclastic of the lot, was Cowell, a Californian. The West Coast, nearer to Asia than Europe, and with a reputation for wacky inventiveness, went on to produce a number of experimental and highly original composers who strayed even further from the European tradition—oddballs such as Alan HOVHANESS (b.1911) and Harry PARTCH (1901–74). There was also one who even called the whole process of composition into question: John CAGE (1912–92).

> **"★"**
>
> **Music and Mushrooms**
>
> Cage was fond of pointing out that the words "mushroom" and "music" are consecutive entries in many dictionaries. As well as his musical achievements, Cage was a well-respected mycologist (mushroom studier), and delighted TV audiences in Italy with regular appearances on a quiz show answering questions on fungi—and performing a few of his own pieces too.

Cage studied for a while with Cowell and Varèse, who encouraged his experimental approach, and with Schoenberg, who didn't—in fact he virtually gave up on Cage as not having a feeling for harmony. That's possibly true, because while Schoenberg's mission was the "emancipation of dissonance," Cage's seemed to be the emancipation of noise. His first published pieces were in his own dissonant style, and were followed by a number of pieces for percussion ensemble (often using "junk" instruments like old car brake drums), which are more concerned with rhythm and time than melody.

John Cage photographed in a typically sunny mood.

126

1961 Robert Redford gets $500 for his first movie, *War Hunt*; he will get $100,000 a day for *A Bridge Too Far*.

1971 Researchers at the University of Nevada succeed in teaching sign language to Washoe, a young female chimp.

1985 A bottle of 1787 Château Lafite owned by Thomas Jefferson, the third American president, fetches $105,000 at auction but proves undrinkable.

He also took Cowell's piano techniques a stage further by inventing the "prepared piano," and as early as 1939 wrote a piece for variable-speed gramophone turntables: this explored sounds that had been previously thought unmusical. These pieces were organized into forms of his own invention, which divide the music into sections of repeating ostinato figures. As often as not, they were written especially to inspire and accompany Merce Cunningham's dance company.

BY CHANCE

In the 1940s Cage studied Eastern philosophies, especially Zen and the I Ching. The idea of "nonintention" appealed, and he tried to find ways of removing himself from the creative process by introducing elements of chance into his music—not just allowing performers to improvise, but using chance and random processes to compose the music. At first he tossed coins to determine what should be written, as in *Music of Changes*, but later he also wrote music with indeterminate outcomes, such as the *Imaginary Landscape No. 4* for 12 radios, and graphic notation intended to be interpreted by the performer.

Cage's aleatoric music (music with some element of chance) became notorious, especially with the composition of *4'33"* four minutes thirty-three seconds of silence. Avant-garde composers in Europe started to introduce aleatoricism into their work, and some, such as the English composer *Cornelius CARDEW* (1936–81), adopted the method wholeheartedly.

By the 1960s, just about anything was acceptable as music, but this posed the question: what next?

Coins tossed to consult the Chinese I Ching became compositional tools in Cage's hands.

Be Prepared
By inserting screws, bolts, and bits of rubber and wood between the strings of a piano to radically alter their sound, Cage invented the "prepared piano." This is played in the normal way via the keyboard, but is in effect a one-man percussion orchestra. Yes, I know it sounds like a crazy idea, but it has an extraordinary range of timbres, and can sound exquisite.

1953 Josef Stalin orders the arrests of certain Kremlin doctors for murdering various Soviet leaders but then dies himself of a brain hemorrhage.

1962 Professor Coon's *The Origin of Races* identifies the world's five basic races; his theory that white races evolved first is used to defend racism.

1981 Odorama; viewers of the spoof soap-opera *Polyester* are provided with scratch 'n' sniff cards to add an extra dimension to their experience.

1955 to the present

Complications
Textures and Complexity

In the 1950s, Eastern European composers started to peek from behind the Iron Curtain. What they found was a revelation to many of them—they were bowled over by the new music starting to filter through. In Poland, Witold LUTOSLAWSKI (1913–94) was one of the first to venture into the realms of the avant-garde, testing the water with a Concerto for Orchestra, influenced by Bartók and Stravinsky, but really plunging in with Venetian Games in 1961. This uses "aleatory counterpoint" (players repeat phrases out of sync with one another in a semirandom way) to create a complex texture where it's difficult (impossible, actually) to hear all the individual lines—more important is the overall effect.

György Ligeti, sophisticated, intricate and witty Hungarian.

And what an effect it had! Young Polish composers loved the dramatic sounds Lutoslawski achieved, and took the idea a step further, composing in great "chunks" of sound within which individual notes are swallowed by the whole. *Krzysztof PENDERECKI'S* (b.1933) *Threnody for the Victims of Hiroshima* is a startling (and intensely moving) example: 52 stringed instruments, each with its own part, play all sorts of string techniques in a bombardment of different "colors."

> **66 ☆ 99**
>
> ### A Batty Transylvanian
>
> Ligeti is quietly proud of being Transylvanian and possesses a delicious and idiosyncratic sense of humor. For a different side of his music, the side that loves cartoons and their busy soundtracks, language and wordplay, and lampooning the musical establishment, try to see (not just hear—because they're theater pieces) *Aventures* and *Nouvelles aventures*. Also worth seeing is the *Poème symphonique*—for an orchestra of 100 metronomes!

CLOCKS AND CLOUDS

Similar things were happening elsewhere. *György LIGETI* (b.1923) fled Budapest after the Russian invasion in 1956 for Vienna and then Cologne, where he came into contact with the likes of Stockhausen and Boulez for the first time. Not content merely to imitate their style, he developed "micropolyphony" (large numbers of

strands of music forming thick clouds of sound), and used mechanically precise rhythmic devices which distort the listener's perception of time (not surprising, then, that he wrote a piece called *Clocks and Clouds*). The result is less dramatic than the work of his Polish contemporaries, with gradual changes from one texture to another, but not without the occasional wild outburst. He is considered the most musical and approachable of modernist composers.

SOUNDS EASY...

Don't be put off by complexity. This "textural" music is very approachable (Ligeti even became popular, for heaven's sake, after Kubrick used bits of his music in *2001: A Space Odyssey*), and easier to get to grips with than most of the avant-garde. Don't worry too much how it's put together (aleatory counterpoint, micropolyphony, or stochastic calculations), what's important is the sound world created.

PROBABLY ...

Another émigré, *Iannis* XENAKIS (b.1922), left his native Greece after the war, having been wounded in the Resistance at the beginning of 1945, and on arriving in Paris in 1947 discovered the European avant-garde. As you might expect from a

A member of the orchestra in Ligeti's *Poème symphonique*.

trained engineer— for a while he collaborated with the architect Le Corbusier —he organizes sounds in mathematical fashion (not as dry as it sounds; it's sensational stuff). Using the theories of probability and statistics to combine aleatoricism with rigid control, he invented what he calls "stochastic" music— hugely complex music in great chunks (sound familiar?). He found this approach suited electronic music well, with computers very useful for doing all the donkey work. All his music, and there's a lot of it, explores in one way or another the connections between music and mathematics: as he himself once said, "We are all Pythagoreans."

1966 A meter reader in Pennsylvania finds the charred leg of 92-year-old Dr. John Bentley, apparently the victim of spontaneous human combustion.

1971 Greenpeace, the environmental campaign group, is founded in Canada by opponents of nuclear testing.

1972 Eight Palestinians break into the Munich Olympic Village, taking nine Israeli athletes hostage and killing two others.

1965 to the present
'Tis a Gift to Be Simple
Minimalism

Meanwhile, back in the States, there was a reaction against the excesses of the avant-garde. The randomness of Cage's aleatoricism and the absolute control of Serialism was all very well, but it wasn't exactly easy listening—in fact the results often sound remarkably similar. Young composers (as always) were looking for something fresh, and what they came up with was Minimalism: music based on a minimum of very simple material, and characterized by constant repetition and very gradual change. Mesmeric stuff that will either send you into a trance or drive you out of your mind.

East and West—the twain meet beautifully in Takemitsu's music.

The inspiration for Minimalism was mainly in the repetitive rhythms and static harmonies of African music, together with the contemplative quality of Asian music, but also had some connections with Satie and especially Cage (you don't get any more minimal than *4'33"*) in their use of exotic, nonprogressive ostinatos. Although Stockhausen's *Klavierstück IX*, with its seemingly endless repetition of one chord, might be described as having Minimalist tendencies, and some of Ligeti's music is based on repetition, *Terry* RILEY (b.1935) was the first true Minimalist composer. His enormously

1974 A Gallup poll reveals that 11 percent of Americans (about 32 million people) claim to have seen UFOs.

1978 Robert Redford, Steve McQueen, Paul Newman, James Caan, and Warren Beatty turn down $4 million to play Superman.

1987 In Britain, a BBC TV weather forecaster ridicules the idea of an imminent hurricane; but 19 people are killed and 15 million trees are blown down.

influential *Keyboard Studies* and *In C* (a very apt title, which sums up the piece) resulted from his studies of non-European music, and messing around with tape loops in a Paris studio in the early 1960s.

The idea caught on in a big way in the U.S. *Philip GLASS* (b.1937) expanded, if that's the right word, the Minimalist style into larger-scale works, even complete operas, using almost no material at all but making it last for literally hours. According to taste you'll think it's marvelously hypnotic or crashingly dull. Rather more sophisticated is the Minimalism of

Steve Reich's music-theater piece *The Cave* —complex minimalism.

Steve REICH (b.1936). Where Riley and Glass achieved gradual change by repeating a figure several times, then making a slight change to the figure and repeating the new figure, and so on, Reich found a means of constant change by "phasing"—repeating figures at very slightly different speeds simultaneously so that the various instruments gradually get out of sync with one another, and the music seems to metamorphose.

A second generation of Minimalists has taken the style just a bit further, introducing elements of jazz and rock and speeding up the pace of harmonic change. *John ADAMS* (b.1947) in particular has gone so far along this road that his music now has minimal connection with its Minimalist roots, becoming almost Romantic in its lushness. Whatever next?

WORKS TO WATCH

Riley's *Keyboard Studies* and *In C* were seminal Minimalist pieces, but perhaps more for their novelty than any musical value. Opinion is evenly divided over Glass's music: it's either pretentiously over-long or hypnotically profound. Try *Music with Changing Parts* or the operas *Einstein on the Beach* or *Akhnaten* and make up your own mind. Reich seems to have won the majority vote in favor with classics such as *Six Pianos*, *Drumming*, *The Desert Music*, *Clapping Music*, and *Different Trains*. And Adams is now one of the most popular living composers; look out for the operas *Nixon in China* and *The Death of Klinghoffer*, the *Grand Pianola Music*, and the orchestral pieces *Shaker Loops*, *Fearful Symmetry*, *Harmonielehre*, and the fanfares *Tromba Lontana* and *Short Ride in a Fast Machine*.

WORKS TO WATCH

It Works Both Ways

Western music has often been influenced by other cultures, for example in the eighteenth-century craze for Turkish" music (think of Mozart's *Turkish Rondo*) and the exotic sounds of Debussy and Messiaen. In the twentieth century, however, increasing numbers of composers brought up in different musical traditions have studied Western music, and achieved a real integration of musical languages. To some extent this can be seen in the music of Kaikhosru Sorabji (1892–1988), but more completely in pieces such as *November Steps* by the Japanese composer Toru Takemitsu (1930–98).

1982 Cambridge scientists, using cell fusion, produce the "geep," a cross between a goat and a sheep.

1982 The Mirage computer system, making screen images fold, revolve, or take on a variety of geometric shapes, is developed in Britain.

1988 For its bicentenary, Australia issues a new $10 bill made of plastic. It is virtually indestructible, surviving boiling, washing, and burial.

2000 and beyond

Where Do We Go from Here?

The Future of Classical Music

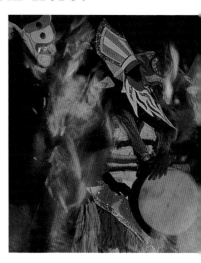

Classical music at the turn of the millennium seems to be in a crisis. Again. Let's face it, it's always been in a crisis—that's the nature of the beast, and what makes it a vital and exciting art form. At any point in musical history, there have been those who have thrown up their hands in horror at the dreadful noise young composers have been trying to palm off as music, but it hasn't ground to a halt yet. And it's never going to.

What form it's going to take next is really anybody's guess—but we can hazard a few predictions, based on what is happening right now. Can current trends develop even further, or are they more likely to provoke an opposite reaction?

Take nationalism, for instance: it stimulated an interest in "exotic" music, starting with Mahler, Debussy, and Ravel, but had run its natural course by mid-century and transformed into a sort of internationalism. Newly-improved communication has brought Western composers in touch with non-European cultures, and vice versa, so most Western composers now use elements of exotic

music in their work, and composers such as Takemitsu have successfully achieved a real blend of East and West. This cross-fertilization seems likely to continue—although who knows, maybe neonationalism is in the cards.

Perhaps the hardiest of the transcultural hybrids is jazz, which has influenced and been influenced by "square" music from the beginning; and, although people are loath to admit it, pop and rock have already started to revitalize the classical music scene. Sometimes it's impossible to make a distinction between them—*Frank* ZAPPA (1940–93), for instance, has (at last!) been accepted by the musical establishment as a

1990 New York purchases 150 miles of inch-wide "ticker-tape" to honor Nelson Mandela; the subsequent cleanup costs $150,000.

1997 The Petronas Towers in Kuala Lumpur, Malaysia, is the tallest building in the world, 88 stories high and yards taller than Chicago's Sears Tower.

1997 Diana Princess of Wales, estranged wife of the heir to the British throne, is killed in a car crash in Paris; millions mourn the death of an icon.

African music is no longer marginalized, but instead has become a major force in Western composition of all kinds of music, including classical.

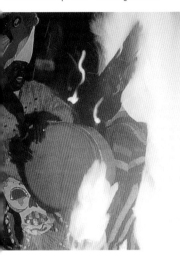

leaving their audiences (and many performers) way behind. Even the mathematical and technical intricacies of Boulez and Xenakis have been exceeded by composers such as *Brian FERNEYHOUGH* (b.1943) and *James DILLON* (b.1950). Very much a minority interest at the moment, but the jury's still out.

During the twentieth century a widening gulf appeared between what the public wanted and what classical composers were producing. The gap, at its worst mid-century, was filled to some extent by jazz and pop, but now the situation seems to be resolving itself. Perhaps audiences are getting more sophisticated (they're certainly bigger than they were a few years ago), or composers less abstruse— whatever it is, there's definitely a growing interest in contemporary music.

I haven't a clue which direction it's going to take next. Maybe there's something completely new just around the corner that nobody's noticed yet. But one thing's for sure—it'll be worth listening to.

significant composer, despite his roots in '60s rock. There'll be more like him.

Minimalism, too, is a result of African and Asian influences, but is losing momentum now. It was, after all, largely a reaction to postwar complexity, and maybe it has run its course. Minimalist composers, notably John Adams, are gradually drifting away from the static quality of the style and rediscovering the inherent tension and resolution of tonality. Perhaps the beginnings of a "Neoromantic" movement may be brewing there.

Meanwhile, some composers have gone down the road of increasing complexity, especially with the aid of computers, often

Vanessa Mae, bringing pop to classical.

Learning the Lingo

A glossary of common musical jargon. Impress your friends and crack those crossword clues.

A CAPPELLA
Of a choir, unaccompanied by instruments.

ADAGIO
Slow. Used as a noun, it means a movement or piece played *adagio*, such as Samuel Barber's *Adagio for Strings*.

ALLEGRO
Fast. *Allegretto* means "a little *allegro*," moderately fast. Both can also be used as nouns, like adagio.

ANDANTE
Moderately slow (it literally means "going"—make of that what you will).

ARPEGGIO
A chord played "like a harp": i.e., the notes sounding one after another in quick succession rather than simultaneously.

CADENCE
A sequence of notes or chords at the end of a phrase of music, analogous to a comma or a period.

CADENZA
The bit in a concerto or aria where soloists show off their technique, without the distraction of accompaniment. Cadenzas are sometimes improvised.

CODA
Literally, "tail"—a bit at the end of a piece or movement that finishes it off neatly.

CON BRIO
With spirit. Possibly Weelkes's downfall (see page 31).

CRESCENDO
Getting louder.

DA CAPO
"From the head." Repeat the music from the beginning, and stop at the instruction *fine* (end).

DIMINUENDO
Getting quieter.

DYNAMICS
How loud or soft the music should be played. Instructions such as *forte* and *piano* are known as dynamic markings.

FANTASIA
Not just a Disney movie. An instrumental piece in a free, improvisatory style, popular in the Renaissance and Baroque periods.

GLISSANDO
"Sliding" from one note to another— usually on the trombone or strings.

INTERVAL

1) The distance between two notes in a scale, such as an octave (i.e., C to C, eight notes) or a fifth (i.e., C to G, five notes).

LARGO

Slow and grand, literally "broad." *Larghetto* means "a little *largo*," presumably not quite as slow or grand. Both can be used as a noun, as in Handel's *Largo*.

LEGATO

Smoothly—the opposite of *staccato*.

LENTO

Slow. Well, very slow, actually— slower than *adagio*.

MODERATO

Moderate (a tempo indication, not an opinion).

ORNAMENT

A little twiddly bit added into a melody, such as a trill. Very popular in the Baroque period.

PIZZICATO

Plucked. Nothing to do with poultry, but an instruction to string players to use their fingers rather than their bows.

PRESTO

Very fast, but not quite as fast as *prestissimo*.

RUBATO

Not strictly with the beat—the performer can shorten or lengthen notes to give further expressive effect. It literally translates as "robbed."

STACCATO

"Detached," each note being cut short— the opposite of *legato*.

SYNCOPATION

Shifting the accent off the main beats of the bar. Syncopation is a vital ingredient in jazz, but is centuries old.

TIMBRE

Tone quality, the distinctive sound of a particular instrument or voice.

TRIAD

A three-note chord made up of two intervals of a third; for example, C-E-G.

TRILL

An ornament (see above), rapidly alternating between a note and the one above.

TUTTI

Literally, "all." An orchestral *tutti* is when everybody is playing.

UNISON

When two instruments or voices are playing the same notes of a melody, they are said to be playing in unison.

VIBRATO

The "wobble" that instrumentalists and singers use to give warmth to a note.

The Art of Listening
How and Where to Listen to Classical Music

Now that you've read all about it, you probably want to put your newfound knowledge to the test. But before you rush to a concert or buy a new recording, let's consider the best way to catch the music you're itching to hear.

Now, I don't want to get too picky about this, but there's a big difference between hearing and listening. The sort of stuff played in supermarkets, euphemistically called "easy listening," has its place (the supermarket, for instance), but it's like aural wallpaper—you hear it, but you don't have to listen too carefully. Classical music demands more concentration, but the rewards are greater. That said, it isn't always possible to give it your full attention, and listening with half an ear while doing the ironing is better than not listening at all.

Ideally, of course, you should go to a concert or recital and catch some real, live music. It's a good night out, and you'll be free to enjoy the music away from the distractions of home (and for Pete's sake, switch off your cell phone or pager). But, much as I love concertgoing, there are drawbacks. If you don't live near a big city, opportunities to hear live music are limited to trips to town, or the occasional touring performers (who tend to play "safe" popular classics). And going to a concert is expensive; for the price of a ticket you could have gotten a CD to add to your collection. All the same, a live concert can't be beat.

So what are the alternatives? Well, for a start there are radio stations devoted to classical music, often broadcasting live

concerts, and of course there are recordings. With modern hi-fi equipment and digitally recorded CDs, the quality is almost better than live, and you can listen whenever you like—and more importantly, as often as you like, so you can really get to know a new piece. The downside is that we all (yup, me too) get a bit lazy about really concentrating and listening, and get involved with something else while the music's playing, a sin compounded by the car stereo system and the Walkman.

Anyway, let's just assume you can make time to listen, really listen, to some music.

Personal stereo systems allow you to choose your own program—and venue.

Start by trying to put the music into context: when it was written, by whom, what style. That kind of background information helps you know what to expect. Find out as much as you can about the piece from program or sleeve notes, which usually point out some of the important features of the music—the number of movements and some indication of their mood (or at least tempo), what form it's in, the instruments or singers in it, that sort of thing. Then just open your ears and try to pick out as many "landmarks" as you can, such as recurring themes, climaxes, changes of mood, whatever strikes you. Then, when you get the chance, listen again (tip: if you're going to a concert, it helps if you can listen to new pieces at home beforehand).

Don't give up if you find it hard going. Keep an open mind, try another time, and you may find you get more out of a piece that you thought was boring or downright incomprehensible. You might still hate it after repeated listening, but chances are it'll grow on you.

For those who can afford it, the thrill of live orchestral music—with a conductor at the helm—is unbeatable.

Performers and Conductors
A Highly Subjective Selection

Sir Thomas Beecham, if not the best, a witty and much-loved conductor.

Before we start, let's get one thing straight—I don't like the trend of idolizing performers. Often the soloist or conductor's name is in larger letters than the composer's on programs and record sleeves, and people pay a fortune to hear, say, Pavarotti, no matter what he's performing. Crazy! When the audience is more aware of the performance than the music, then I think something's wrong.

Having said that, there are some superb interpreters about—and some dreadful ones. To some extent it's a matter of taste, but there are some objective criteria: accuracy, technique, sensitivity, and so on. A lot of performers tend to specialize in a particular type of music, too, so sometimes their Bach is worse than their Scheidt.

Let's start with conductors. For precision, clarity, and attention to detail, especially in twentieth-century music, Pierre Boulez—at his best with the BBC Symphony Orchestra—can't be beat. Just as rigorous technically, but more flamboyant on the podium, is Simon Rattle, particularly with the Birmingham Symphony Orchestra. Then there's Seiji Ozawa, a really good all-arounder who

has brought out the best in the Boston Symphony Orchestra, and for "authentic" performance, try Roger Norrington or John Eliot Gardiner. And my all-time favorite? Thomas Beecham, of course, for his highly individual sense of humor as much as his skill as a conductor.

Chamber groups are a bit more personal, and I'm bound to ruffle a few feathers, but here goes: the Amadeus String Quartet (sadly disbanded in 1987) has to be high on the list, especially for the classical repertoire, closely followed by the Lindsay Quartet (or Lindsays: the affectionate abbreviation is now officially adopted), more for Beethoven and the twentieth-century repertoire. There's also the quirky American Kronos Quartet, who specialize in contemporary stuff, and Fretwork, a consort of viols who play modern and early music—and while we're in that area, look

out for the Hilliard Ensemble's superb performances of medieval and Renaissance choral music. And for championing the cause of new music, and with brilliance, I give full marks to Ensemble Modern and Ensemble Intercontemporain (but couldn't they have found a snappier name?).

Without getting into the realms of hero worship, I do quietly enthuse about some soloists too, for their musicianship more than their technical brilliance. My number-one favorite has to be Alfred Brendel—not a flashy pianist, but so good he lets the music speak, as does the cellist Heinrich Schiff (especially in the Bach solo cello suites); there's also the eccentric pianist Glenn Gould (died in 1982, but there are plenty of recordings), whom you'll either love or hate. For something out of the ordinary, there's the trumpeter Håkan Hardenberger or the amazing percussionist Evelyn Glennie.

What about singers? Well, to be honest, I can't stand most of them—but notable exceptions include Emma Kirkby and Dietrich Fischer-Dieskau (the latter especially with the late Gerald Moore, the greatest of all accompanists), simply because they treat singing as an art, not an ego trip or a competitive sport.

The Hilliard Ensemble, masters of early choral music.

Chronology

c.995–after 1033	Guido d'Arezzo	*Italian*
1098–1179	Hildegard of Bingen	*German*
c.1160–1205	Pérotin	*French*
c.1135–1201	Léonin	*French*
c.1245–c.1288	Adam de la Halle	*French*
1291–1361	Vitry, Philippe de	*French*
c.1300–77	Machaut, Guillaume de	*French*
c.1325–97	Landini, Francesco	*Italian*
c.1390–c.1453	Dunstable, John	*English*
c.1397–1474	Dufay, Guillaume	*French*
c.1400–60	Binchois, Gilles de Bins *dit*	*Franco-Flemish*
c.1410–c.1497	Ockeghem, Johannes	*Franco-Flemish*
c.1440–1521	Josquin Des Préz	*Northern French*
c.1490–1545	Taverner, John	*English*
c.1490–1562	Willaert, Adrian	*Flemish*
1494–1576	Sachs, Hans	*German*
c.1505–68	Arcadelt, Jacob	*Flemish*
c.1505–85	Tallis, Thomas	*English*
c.1510–c.1556	Clemens non Papa, Jacobus	*Franco-Flemish*
1510–66	Cabézon, Antonio de	*Spanish*
1525–94	Palestrina, Giovanni da	*Italian*
1532–94	Lassus, Orlando di	*Franco-Flemish*
c.1510–85	Gabrieli, Andrea	*Italian*
1543–1623	Byrd, William	*English*
1548–1611	Victoria, Tomás Luis de	*Spanish*
c.1554/6–1612	Gabrieli, Giovanni	*Italian*
1557/8–1602	Morley, Thomas	*English*
c.1560–1613	Gesualdo, Don Carlo	*Italian*
1561–1633	Peri, Jacopo	*Italian*
c.1562–1621	Sweelinck, Jan	*Netherlands*
c.1562–1628	Bull, John	*English*
1563–1626	Dowland, John	*English*
1567–1643	Monteverdi, Claudio	*Italian*
1576–1623	Weelkes, Thomas	*English*
1582–1652	Allegri, Gregorio	*Italian*
1583–1625	Gibbons, Orlando	*English*
1583–1643	Frescobaldi, Girolamo	*Italian*
1585–1672	Schütz, Heinrich	*German*
1602–76	Cavalli, Pietro Francesco	*Italian*
1605–74	Carissimi, Giacomo	*Italian*
1623–1669	Cesti, Antonio	*Italian*
1632–87	Lully, Jean-Baptiste	*Italian/French*
c.1637–1707	Buxtehude, Dietrich	*Danish/German*
1645–1704	Charpentier, Marc-Antoine	*French*
1649–1708	Blow, John	*English*
1653–1713	Corelli, Archangelo	*Italian*
1659–95	Purcell, Henry	*English*
1660–1725	Scarlatti, Alessandro	*Italian*

1668–1733	Couperin, François	*French*
1671–1751	Albinoni, Tomaso Giovanni	*Italian*
c.1674–1707	Clarke, Jeremiah	*English*
1678–1741	Vivaldi, Antonio	*Italian*
1681–1767	Telemann, Georg Philipp	*German*
1683–1764	Rameau, Jean-Philippe	*French*
1685–1750	Bach, Johann Sebastian	*German*
1685–1757	Scarlatti, Domenico	*Italian*
1685–1759	Handel, George Frideric	*German/English*
1710–78	Arne, Thomas Augustine	*English*
1710–36	Pergolesi, Giovanni	*Italian*
1710–84	Bach, Wilhelm Friedemann	*German*
1711–79	Boyce, William	*English*
1714–87	Gluck, Christoph Willibald	*Bohemian-German*
1714–88	Bach, Carl Philipp Emanuel	*German*
1717–57	Stamitz, Johann Wenzel	*Bohemian*
1732–1809	Haydn, Franz Josef	*Austrian*
1735–82	Bach, Johann Christian	*German*
1743–1805	Boccherini, Luigi	*Italian*
1750–1825	Salieri, Antonio	*Italian*
1756–91	Mozart, Wolfgang Amadeus	*Austrian*
1760–1842	Cherubini, Luigi	*Italian*
1770–1827	Beethoven, Ludwig van	*German*
1778–1837	Hummel, Johann Nepomuk	*Austrian*
1782–1840	Paganini, Niccolò	*Italian*
1786–1826	Weber, Carl Maria von	*German*
1792–1868	Rossini, Gioachino	*Italian*
1797–1828	Schubert, Franz	*Austrian*
1797–1848	Donizetti, Gaetano	*Italian*
1801–35	Bellini, Vincenzo	*Italian*
1803–69	Berlioz, Hector	*French*
1804–57	Glinka, Mikhail	*Russian*
1804–49	Strauss, Johann I	*Austrian*
1809–47	Mendelssohn [-Bartholdy], Felix	*German*
1810–49	Chopin, Fryderyk Franciszek [Frédéric]	*Polish*
1810–56	Schumann, Robert	*German*
1811–86	Liszt, Franz	*Hungarian*
1813–1901	Verdi, Giuseppe	*Italian*
1813–69	Dargomizhsky, Alexander	*Russian*
1813–83	Wagner, Richard	*German*
1818–93	Gounod, Charles François	*French*
1819–80	Offenbach, Jacques	*German/French*
1819–96	Schumann, Clara	*German*
1822–90	Franck, César	*Belgian*
1824–84	Smetana, Bedřich	*Czech*
1824–96	Bruckner, Anton	*Austrian*
1825–99	Strauss, Johann II	*Austrian*
1826–64	Foster, Stephen Collins	*U.S.*

1829-69	Gottschalk, Louis Moreau	*U.S.*
1833-87	Borodin, Alexander	*Russian*
1833-97	Brahms, Johannes	*German*
1835-1918	Cui, César	*Russian*
1835-1921	Saint-Saëns, Camille	*French*
1837-1910	Balakirev, Mily Alexeyevich	*Russian*
1838-75	Bizet, Georges	*French*
1839-81	Mussorgsky, Modest	*Russian*
1840-93	Tchaikovsky, Pyotr Il'yich	*Russian*
1841-1904	Dvořák, Antonin	*Czech*
1843-1907	Grieg, Edvard	*Norwegian*
1844-1908	Rimsky-Korsakov, Nicolay Andreyevich	*Russian*
1844-1937	Widor, Charles Marie	*French*
1845-1924	Fauré, Gabriel-Urbain	*French*
1851-1931	Indy, Vincent d'	*French*
1854-1928	Janáček, Leoš	*Czech*
1854-1932	Sousa, John Philip	*U.S.*
1857-1934	Elgar, Sir Edward	*English*
1858-1924	Puccini, Giacomo	*Italian*
1858-1944	Smyth, Dame Ethel	*English*
1860-1903	Wolf, Hugo	*Austrian*
1860-1909	Albéniz, Isaac	*Spanish*
1860-1911	Mahler, Gustav	*Bohemian-Austrian*
1860-1941	Paderewski, Ignacy Jan	*Polish*
1860-1956	Charpentier, Gustave	*French*
1862-1918	Debussy, Claude	*French*
1862-1934	Delius, Frederick	*English*
1864-1949	Strauss, Richard	*German*
1865-1931	Nielsen, Carl	*Danish*
1865-1935	Dukas, Paul	*French*
1865-1936	Glazunov, Alexander	*Russian*
1865-1957	Sibelius, Jean	*Finnish*
1866-1924	Busoni, Ferruccio	*German-Italian*
1866-1925	Satie, Erik	*French*
1868-1917	Joplin, Scott	*U.S.*
1872-1915	Skryabin [Scriabin], Alexander	*Russian*
1872-1958	Vaughan Williams, Ralph	*English*
1873-1916	Reger, Max	*German*
1873-1943	Rachmaninov, Sergey	*Russian*
1874-1934	Holst, Gustav	*English*
1874-1951	Schoenberg, Arnold	*Austro-Hungariann*
1874-1954	Ives, Charles	*U.S.*
1875-1937	Ravel, Maurice	*French*
1876-1946	Falla, Manuel de	*Spanish*
1876-1972	Brian, Havergal	*English*
1881-1945	Bartók, Béla	*Hungarian*
1882-1961	Grainger, Percy	*Australian/American*
1882-1967	Kodály, Zoltán	*Hungarian*
1882-1971	Stravinsky, Igor	*Russian/French/U.S.*
1883-1945	Webern, Anton von	*Austrian*
1883-1965	Varèse, Edgard	*French/U.S.*
1885-1935	Berg, Alban	*Austrian*
1885-1947	Russolo, Luigi	*Italian*
1887-1959	Villa-Lobos, Heitor	*Brazilian*
1891-1953	Prokofiev, Sergey	*Russian*
1892-1955	Honegger, Arthur	*Swiss*
1892-1974	Milhaud, Darius	*French*
1892-1983	Tailleferre, Germaine	*French*
1892-1988	Sorabji, Kaikhosru	*English*
1895-1963	Hindemith, Paul	*German*
1895-1982	Orff, Carl	*German*
1898-1937	Gershwin, George	*U.S.*
1899-1963	Poulenc, Francis	*French*
1899-1983	Auric, Georges	*French*
1900-50	Weill, Kurt	*German*
1900-90	Copland, Aaron	*U.S.*
b.1901	Rodrigo, Joaquin	*Spanish*
1902-83	Walton, Sir William	*English*
1903-78	Khachaturian, Aram Il'yich	*Armenian*
1904-75	Dallapiccola, Luigi	*Italian*
1905-98	Tippett, Sir Michael	*English*
1906-75	Shostakovich, Dmitri	*Russian*
1906-83	Lutyens, Elisabeth	*English*
b.1908	Carter, Elliott	*U.S.*
1908-92	Messiaen, Olivier	*French*
1910-81	Barber, Samuel	*U.S.*
1912-92	Cage, John	*U.S.*
1913-76	Britten, Baron Benjamin	*English*
1913-94	Lutosławski, Witold	*Polish*
b.1916	Babbitt, Milton	*U.S.*
1918-90	Bernstein, Leonard	*U.S.*
b.1922	Xenakis, Iannis	*Greek-Romanian/French*
b.1923	Ligeti, György	*Hungarian/Austrian*
1924-90	Nono, Luigi	*Italian*
b.1925	Berio, Luciano	*Italian*
b.1925	Boulez, Pierre	*French*
b.1926	Henze, Hans Werner	*German*
b.1928	Stockhausen, Karlheinz	*German*
1930-96	Takemitsu, Toru	*Japanese*
b.1933	Penderecki, Krzysztof	*Polish*
1934-98	Schnittke, Alfred	*Russian*
b.1934	Maxwell Davies, Sir Peter	*English*
b.1934	Birtwistle, Harrison	*English*
b.1935	Pärt, Arvo	*Estonian*
b.1935	Riley, Terry	*U.S.*
b.1936	Reich, Steve	*U.S.*
b.1937	Glass, Philip	*U.S.*
1940-93	Zappa, Frank	*U.S.*
b.1943	Bryars, Gavin	*English*
b.1944	Tavener, John	*English*
b.1947	Adams, John	*U.S.*
b.1944	Nyman, Michael	*English*

Index